THE COMPLETING MINISTRY OF PAUL

MESSAGE ONE

THE HEAVENLY CALLING OF PAUL

Scripture Reading: Acts 9:1-15; 26:13-19; Gal. 1:11-17; 2:20; 3:27; 4:19; Col. 1:24-29

THE NEED FOR PAUL'S MINISTRY

Without Paul's completing ministry, there is no way for Christ's heavenly ministry to be carried out. Of course, without Christ's heavenly ministry Paul's ministry would have no ground. These two ministries work together — the one in the heavens and the other within us. Paul's ministry reflected what Christ was ministering in the heavens.

Christ's heavenly ministry began in Acts 2. Between chapters two and nine Christ's ministry was proceeding, but Paul's had not yet begun. Something was missing. Yes, Peter was ministering, but if we compare his ministry with Paul's, we shall sense a lack. In Acts 9 the story of Paul's momentous conversion is recorded, a conversion that was brought about, not by any human being, but by the direct intervention of the Lord Jesus from the heavens.

A CALLING FROM THE HEAVENS

In Hebrews 3:1 Paul calls the Hebrews to whom he was writing "partakers of a heavenly calling." The word heavenly shows that Paul's calling was specific. Those Hebrews were companions in receiving the heavenly calling.

This was not a calling on earth. Consider, in contrast to Paul, how Peter was called. Peter was at the Sea of Galilee, fishing with his brother, when a Man from Nazareth came by and called them. "Come, follow Me, and I will make you fishers of men," the Lord Jesus told them (Matt. 4:18-19). How much I loved this story when I was young! I longed also to be a fisher of men. How much better to be a fisher of men rather than a fisher of fish!

After we consider Paul's calling, however, we shall see that there is no comparison between the two. Peter's calling was marvelous, but it was simple and from this earth. Peter was called by the Lord Jesus in His incarnation. That call is easy to understand. Paul's calling, on the other hand, is beyond our comprehension. The call to Saul of Tarsus came from the heavens, not from the Jesus on this earth, but from the ascended, glorified One in the heavens.

Saul of Tarsus was one of a strong character. He was happily nearing the end of his journey from Jerusalem to Damascus, eager to arrive and fulfill his task of arresting all those who believed in Jesus. It was midday as he approached Damascus. Suddenly "there shone from heaven a great light round about" him (Acts 22:6). He fell to the ground and heard a voice saying, "Saul, Saul, why persecutest thou me?" (v. 7). He must have thought, "What do you mean? I have been persecuting Peter, and John, and Stephen. But all those whom I have persecuted were on the earth. I have never harmed anyone in the heavens. Who can this be, saying that I am persecuting him?"

So he asked. Calling this unseen One Lord, he said, "Who art thou, Lord?" (v. 8). The answer came, "I am Jesus!" Saul must have been filled with consternation. Jesus was crucified and buried. How could He be speaking from the heavens? How could He be alive?

Such was the calling of Paul. All mysterious!

THE GOSPEL PREACHED TO PAUL

Paul's completing ministry is to tell us that God is through with religion. Religion is an enemy to God's economy. Have you ever heard the gospel preached with this as its message? You have no doubt heard that God condemns you because of your sinfulness and worldliness. Have you ever been told that you must get out of religion?

that religion is God's enemy? What you have heard as the gospel is not the completing ministry. The gospel pertains not merely to sin and the world. What God wants is not religion. He wants His Son revealed in you (Gal. 1:16). This is the completing ministry. At the time of Saul's calling he was not gambling nor cheating others. He was an upright, honest man. He could say of himself, "As to the righteousness which is in the law, become blameless" (Phil. 3:6).

But Saul was altogether in religion. He needed to be rescued. He needed revelation. Why did the Lord Jesus come to preach the gospel directly to Saul? Peter, James, and John all knew how to preach the gospel. Their preaching, however, was to sinners. They would not have known how to preach the gospel to such a zealous religionist as Saul. What was the gospel message Saul heard from the Lord Jesus? A light from heaven first made him fall to the ground. Then a voice asked, "Why are you persecuting Me?" When Saul replied, "Who are You, Lord?" the voice answered, "I am Jesus, whom you are persecuting."

Could Peter have preached such a gospel? No! Only Christ Himself could. In his own sight Saul of Tarsus was not sinful or against God; he was zealous for God and righteous according to the law. Yet actually he was against God and His economy. God's economy is that we forsake the law and religion and have His Son revealed in us. At the time when Saul was called, however, Peter did not clearly realize this. John and James did not know this in a full way either. Thus the Lord Jesus Himself had to touch Saul directly.

THE NEED FOR PAUL'S MINISTRY

Why was the Lord after Saul? The Lord needed an apostle to complete His revelation. There may be many preachings, but they do not adequately complete God's revelation. The purpose of Paul's calling was to get the one person who could complete that revelation (Col. 1:25).

Without Paul's ministry, what would we lack? We would have the thirty-nine books of the Old Testament and at least the four Gospels in the New. What would we be missing?

Firstly, we would not realize that Christ is in us, that He must live in us and be our life and life supply. In the other forty-three books this point is not clearly stressed. Of course, John's Gospel mentions that we must abide in Him and He in us (John 15:4) and that because He lives, we also shall live (14:19). Without Paul's writings, however, these words would not be easy to understand. It is Paul who tells us that Christ must live in us, must live in our spirit, and be in us as the life-giving Spirit. He is our life, even our life supply, and is Himself to be formed in us.

Secondly, Paul's writings reveal Christ as the all-inclusive One. No other books of the Bible reveal Christ as the embodiment of God, as the Firstborn of all creation, as the Firstborn from among the dead, and as the reality of all positive things.

Thirdly, only in Paul's writings do we find Christ as the Head and the church as the Body. This thought was not there before Paul's ministry. It is his Epistles which develop this truth.

These three points are the completion of God's revelation. Because of Paul's writings, we know that Christ in us is the hope of glory, that Christ is the all-inclusive One, and that the church is the Body and Christ the Head.

I hope that now we can all see how significant Paul's calling is. Peter was called to be a fisher of men, but Paul was called to complete the revelation of God. There is no comparison. The Catholic Church may exalt Peter, but he was after all only a fisherman! I am more appreciative of Paul.

THE GREATNESS OF OUR LATER CALLING

Our calling is like his. We were not called by the earthly Jesus during His incarnation. Our calling came from the ascended, exalted Jesus, not from the Sea of Galilee but from the heavens!

It is a principle that the one who is born later is greater. You recall the Lord's words concerning John the Baptist: "Truly I say to you, Among those born of women, there has not arisen a greater than John the Baptist; yet he who is smallest in the kingdom of the heavens is greater than he" (Matt. 11:11). Though John was greater than all the prophets of the past, he was inferior to a little one in the kingdom of the heavens. Do you consider yourself greater than Adam, and Abraham, and Moses? You are greater than all of them, because you came later! The later, the greater! The earlier ones are in the initial stage, but now you are in the completing stage.

From Adam to Abraham there were two thousand years. From Abraham to Christ were another two thousand years. Now from Christ to us there are another two thousand years. Surely we agree that the first and second set of two thousand years were not all that great. Even in the third two thousand years those born at the beginning were not as blessed as are we who were born at the end! Why are we the most blessed? It is because we stand upon the shoulders of all those who have gone before. Noah stood upon the shoulders of Adam. Abraham was upon the shoulders of Noah. Moses was upon Abraham. Then the New Testament saints are upon the shoulders of those from the Old. Today we stand upon the shoulders of Peter, Paul, and Martin Luther! To tell the truth, I wish I had come along later! Then I could stand upon your shoulders; as it is, you are upon mine!

You are in the time of the completing of the Lord's economy. The Lord's recovery today is completing His economy. Before you came into the recovery, I doubt that you saw much of these three matters: Christ in you as the hope of glory, Christ all in all, and the church as the Body with Christ as the Head. For over fifty years I have been in the recovery. My time is nearing the end. There is still something which needs completing. This will fall upon your shoulders. You will continue this completing ministry, which consists primarily of these three items we have mentioned.

CHRIST IN US

Paul said that it pleased God to reveal His Son in him (Gal. 1:15-16). At the time of his conversion, God was happy to reveal Christ in Paul. In our gospel preaching we must tell people not merely that they are sinners in need of Jesus and that they must repent before God. They also need to know that Jesus must come into them as their life. They need Him to live in them. Without this in our gospel preaching, it is incomplete.

Saul of Tarsus, as we have said, was not a sinful person. He was not an idol worshipper. But though he was blameless and zealous for God, he did not have Christ in him. At the time of his conversion, God specifically revealed His Son in him. From then on, Paul was different. He realized that what mattered was not the law, nor the worship of God, nor good works. Rather, he must have Christ as a living Person in him.

The second of the Triune God must enter into our being. Another Person, a divine Person, must come into us, to be our life and our life supply; to be formed in us; to be one with us, even to become us; and to make us one with Him, even to become Him!

Sometimes Christians ask new ones, "Are you saved? Have you been regenerated? Have you received the Holy Ghost?" I heard such questions asked even fifty years ago. But never once did I hear the question, "Do you have the Son of God living in you?" It would be good to ask people this. The central point of the gospel is that the Son of God comes into you as your Person. If your gospel preaching misses this, you have not preached in a full way.

THE ALL-INCLUSIVE CHRIST

How did the Lord Jesus indicate to Paul at his conversion that He was all-inclusive? When He called to him from the heavens, "Why do you persecute Me?" He was implying that all those whom Saul had been persecuting were part of Him. Peter, James, and Stephen were included in Him. For Saul to persecute them was to persecute Jesus.

In Saul's thinking Jesus of Nazareth was a man on this earth who had been crucified and buried. To his astonishment this very One came to him from the heavens! Here is a further indication that Christ is all-inclusive. Not only are all His disciples included in Him. He is also present everywhere. He is on the earth, but He is also in the heavens.

What a marvelous gospel message the Lord Jesus preached to Saul! The words were simple, the sentences short. But how much they implied! Saul realized that this One whom he had been resisting was all-inclusive. He was every one of His believers, and He was everywhere, both in heaven and on earth. Saul recognized he could not escape from this all-inclusive, all-present One.

THE HEAD AND HIS BODY

How did Saul learn at his conversion that the church is the Body of Christ? Again, the Lord's words, "Why do you persecute *Me*?" caused him to realize that the believers were one with Christ. Saul may have thought, "I have not been persecuting anyone in the heavens," but the Lord was indicating to him that those whom he had been persecuting were members of His Body. Because they were one with Him, for Saul to touch them was to touch the Head. Suppose I beat someone on the arm. He will protest, "Why are you beating me?" If I reply, "I am not beating you. I am beating your arm," he will no doubt say, "Look, if you beat my arm, you are beating me," because the arm is a member of his body. Similarly, from the Lord's words Saul could infer that all the believers were the members of Christ.

After Saul realized who was speaking to him, he raised a second question, "Lord, what wilt thou have me to do?" (Acts 9:6). "And the Lord said unto him, Arise, and go into the city, and it shall be told thee what thou must do." The Lord by this word was indicating that Saul could no longer be individualistic. He was to go into Damascus, where his next step would be shown him by an otherwise unknown believer named Ananias. Now that Saul had been brought into the Body, if he wanted to know the Lord's will, he must go through a member of the Body rather than be told directly by the Head.

Do you see how marvelous a conversion Paul's was? Peter was merely told, "Follow Me, and I will make you fishers of men." Paul's case was not that simple. With his calling there are indications of Christ in me, Christ all-inclusive, and Christ the Head with the church as His Body. These became the very three things he preached. Without Paul's completing ministry of these three things, there would be no completion to God's revelation. These three crucial points are the components of Paul's ministry.

When we see how precious these are, we shall thank the Lord for bringing us into the recovery. We shall realize that it is here that there is the completing ministry. What Paul preached long ago is being recovered. Hallelujah for the completing ministry — Christ in me the hope of glory! Christ the all-inclusive One! Christ the Head of the Body and the church, the Body of Christ!

A message given by Witness Lee
in Stuttgart, Germany, April 5, 1980

Published by
Living Stream Ministry
1853 W. Ball Road, Anaheim, CA 92804, U.S.A.
(714) 991-4681

THE COMPLETING MINISTRY OF PAUL

MESSAGE TWO

CHRIST LIVING IN ME

Scripture Reading: Gal. 1:13-16; 2:20; 3:27, 28; 4:19; Col. 1:25-27; 3:3, 4, 8-10; 2 Cor. 13:5; Phil. 1:21; Eph. 3:17

As we said in the previous message, there are three crucial points to Paul's ministry. The first of these, which we shall consider in this message, is Christ living within us. The other two we shall cover in subsequent messages.

PLANNED IN ETERNITY

That Christ should live in us was purposed and planned by God in eternity. According to Ephesians 3, in eternity past God planned to work Himself into His chosen people. His eternal purpose is to have a people with Him as life. God will be within them and they will be one with Him. This people will be the Body of Christ to express God Himself in Christ. First they are the church and eventually the New Jerusalem.

The Bible tells us that in eternity past there was only God. Then He purposed to have a Body for Christ. For this He created the universe and then man, the center of the universe. Man, Genesis 1:26 tells us, was made in a specific way. He was made in God's image and according to His likeness. Why was it that God made man in His own form? It was because God intended that one day He would enter man to make man His container, with Himself as the content. From the very beginning, then, from the time of man's creation, the preparation was made for man to contain God.

A VESSEL

Romans 9:20-21 says that man is a vessel. The purpose of a vessel is to contain something. Man is not called an instrument. He was not made to do something, the way a hammer can be used to hit a nail. When the Lord talked to Ananias about Paul, He said, "He is a chosen vessel unto me" (Acts 9:15). Paul was not chosen to be an instrument to finish a work. He was chosen to be a vessel to contain God in Christ, even to the distant parts of the earth.

Later, Paul himself used this same word. "We have this treasure in earthen vessels" (2 Cor. 4:7). We are only an earthen vessel, but within us is the treasure. The treasure is the Triune God. It is Christ Jesus. It is the all-inclusive Spirit. Paul was the leading vessel, the pattern vessel. When Christians study the Bible, they may be impressed with how much work Paul accomplished. In a sense Paul did accomplish a tremendous work. His work, however, was to contain the Lord and then bring the Lord to others; it was not to do a work as such. Wherever he went, he ministered the Lord to people, not in the way of working but rather by containing Him and then sharing Him. He was a vessel containing the Lord and bringing the Lord to others.

CHRIST REVEALED IN US

"It pleased God," Paul tells of the time of his conversion, "to reveal His Son in me" (Gal. 1:15-16). God was pleased to do this one thing: to reveal His Son in Paul. Before God called him, Saul was already a chosen vessel, but he was empty. Even so, he was occupied by the religion of his fathers. His being was full of the law and the traditions. He thought highly of himself. Peter he may have considered an ignorant fisherman from Galilee. But he himself was filled with the law of Moses and the traditions of his people. Much of the day he was no doubt thinking about God and considering how to serve Him. Yet he was void of God, empty, even while being so occupied by the law. He was being misused, usurped, by what was not God's purpose.

God does not want a people who are religious or even sinless. Saul considered himself blameless, yet he was void of Christ. He was zealous for God, yet God was not in him. God's eternal purpose is not to gain a people who will keep the law. He is after a people who are full of Christ.

While Saul was empty, yet so occupied, this dear Lord came, not only to save him, but especially to fill him. On the way to Damascus the Lord called him by name. When Saul replied, "Who art thou, Lord?" the Lord entered into him. It was enough for him to say "Lord." If you want to take a picture with a camera, you simply activate the shutter. With a touch the light gets in and the picture is taken. The moment Saul called "Lord," the shutter opened, even without his realizing it, and the Lord Jesus came in.

You may wonder if Paul was referring to the time of his conversion when he says, "It pleased God . . . to reveal His Son in me." This is clear from the context: "When it pleased God, who set me apart from my mother's womb and called me through His grace, to reveal His Son in me, that I might preach Him among the nations, immediately I did not confer with flesh and blood" (Gal. 1:15-16). Was there any other juncture in Paul's life when God revealed His Son in Paul? To me it is clear that this was the time God revealed His Son to him. This camera had been shut for years. He would not open up, though God as the heavenly light was watching and waiting. Then the Lord came and asked Saul why he was persecuting Him. As soon as the word "Lord" came out in Saul's reply, the shutter was activated and the Son of God was revealed in him. Of course, it was not till later that he realized what had happened.

This is our own story too. When we repented and believed, we may have prayed, "Lord, I am sinful. Have mercy on me and save me." We had no intention of receiving the Lord into us. Our prayer was for the Lord to forgive us and save us, to take care of our troubles. We did not realize when we called "Lord" that we activated the shutter. It took a few days perhaps before we discovered that Somebody was inside us. Before calling on His name, we were alone. Now, however, we find there is Someone in us, not only with us, but in us! Is this not our experience? Especially do we find this is so if we feel like doing something that pertains to the old life. Suppose, for example, we feel like going to a movie. Another One within us says, "I don't feel good about this." While we are saying, "It would be fun to go to a movie," Someone else within is saying, "Better not go!" Who is this One? It is the Son of God revealed in us. He was revealed in us while we were unaware. Aware or not, He came in! Now we cannot get rid of Him. The more we call on Him, whether positively or negatively, the more we become involved with Him. We may say, "Lord, I have had enough of You. Leave me alone. At least give me this weekend for myself. I have something to do." The more we talk to Him this way, the more He bothers us. It is better not to call! If we want to avoid "trouble," we had better not talk to Him! This may help, but I doubt it! Jesus is no longer just a man. He is the ascended Christ. He is the ascended Lord. He is also the all-inclusive Spirit. When we call His name, we get the Person. To call "Jesus" is to activate the shutter. The heavenly light comes in.

Suppose, to use an example, I need one of you. As soon as I call your name, you come. But suppose I do not want you to come. I do not want to have you around. Then it is better simply not to mention your name. If I keep saying, "So-and-so, So-and-so, I do not want you here. Go away, So-and-so, and leave me alone!" it is likely you will stay around.

The Lord is real and living. He is present and near. When we call, "Lord!" He comes at once. I have learned to apply this lesson in preaching the gospel. People may argue and resist what we say, but if we want to win them, the best way is to induce them to call "Lord Jesus."

At the beginning of this message I have listed the verses in Paul's writings that mention Christ living in us. Paul tells us that while he was deep in zeal for religion and the law, the Lord Himself came. From the moment the Lord called him, "Saul, Saul . . . ," he could not get away. It was then that Christ was revealed into him (Gal. 1:13-16).

CHRIST LIVING IN US

"It is no longer I who live, but Christ lives in me" (Gal. 2:20). It is extraordinary to say that another person lives in us. Another Person lives in us! He is not only with us, but in us! If we are students, we may have a roommate living with us. If we are married, we have a wife or husband living with us. But they do not live *in* us! They could never live in us! Nonetheless, we who are saved do have a Person living in us. And not a small person. This One is a great, all-inclusive, divine Person!

Do you realize that there is a living Person in you? It was not simply a piece of bread which got into you, but a living Person! "No longer I . . . but Christ!" Do you know that Christ is in you not only as your life, but as your person as well? Day after day, morning and evening, hour by hour, this Person is in you. This is what Paul tells us in this verse.

CHRIST FORMED IN US

He further says, "My children, of whom I am again in travail until Christ is formed in you" (Gal. 4:19). This Christ has to be formed in us. He may be in us, but limited, restricted, frustrated. For Him to be formed in us means that He occupies us in full. From our spirit, He takes over our mind, our will, and our emotion, thus occupying our whole being. He is in every part of our inner being.

CHRIST AS OUR LIVING

In Philippians 1:21 Paul says, "To me to live is Christ." What a word is this! Paul and Christ lived together as one person. Paul's life was to live Christ. He was one with Christ both in life and in living. He and Christ had one life and one living. Christ lived within him as his life, and he lived Christ without as his living.

CHRIST MAKING HOME IN US

Then Paul prays in Ephesians 3:17, "That Christ may make His home in your hearts." Not only is there a Person in you, but a home built up in you as well. Surely this will be a further bother! Yes, to believe in the Lord Jesus is good. But you will have problems! Another Person comes into you. Do you really like having another Person with you all the time? Then, if you allow Him, He will build a home in you. Do you not agree that this will mean even more "trouble"? He is already within you, and you cannot get Him to leave. Then He wants to settle down and make a home in you. Christ wants to make His home in your heart!

THE GOSPEL

Dear saints, this is the gospel. Our destiny is to contain Christ. For this we were created. It is not up to us. God has created us in this way. Christ must occupy us. Our destiny is to be filled with Him. The gospel is simply this living, all-inclusive Person. He is both God and man. He must fill us!

Satan caused man to fall. The fall brought man to sin and to the world. There were some who turned away from sin and from the world back to God. But halfway back they were held up. What made them come short? Religion. Saul of Tarsus was one of these. Saul turned from sin and from the world. His intention was to return to God, yet religion held him back. Many Christians today are like this. They have turned from sin and the world, with the intention of going to God, but they have been held back by religion. Christ does not fill them. The Lord's recovery would rescue such ones, help them get free of the hook of religion, and lead them on directly to God so that Christ can fill them. In the recovery there is nothing to hold anyone back. All the time we are being urged to go directly to Christ in an inward way, to let Him occupy our whole being, that we may be one with Him and have Him one with us. What a declaration Paul could make: "To me to live is Christ"! All of us must be able to say this, not merely the words but the words backed by the fact. We must be able to tell the whole universe, "To me to live is Christ!" Without this point the divine revelation is not complete.

THE NEED FOR COMPLETION

Even as you read this message, you may still have this need of completion. You have turned back from sin and the world with the intention of going to God. Yet you have gone only halfway. Something close to God, not sinful or worldly in your eyes, is holding you back. You are behind in God's revelation. He would have Christ occupy you in full so that you are able to say, "To me to live is Christ." Until you can truly say this, you are behind in God's full revelation. Thus you need the completing ministry. This completing is Christ as a living Person entering into you, filling you, making Himself one with you, and making your living to be Himself.

What I am saying is all in the Bible. Why are God's people so unaware of this? One day by His mercy I saw these things. Though I was brought up in Christianity, I had never been told about Christ living in me. When the Lord opened my eyes, I could not contain myself. I had to bring this message from the Far East to the western world. You are behind in God's revelation. You are behind! You need the completion! Christ in you, the hope of glory (Col. 1:27)! God destined you not to go to heaven but to contain Christ! Your destiny is to contain Christ and to have Him fill you. With Christ in you, you have the real hope and the real glory.

Can you declare that for you to live is Christ? Is Christ in you? Is He filling you? Has He occupied you? What a high gospel this is!

Of all the books in the Bible, it is Paul's writings which tell us most clearly that Christ lives in us. No wonder his ministry is the completing ministry (Col. 1:25)! God was pleased to reveal His Son in us. Now it is no longer we who live, but Christ lives in us. He is being formed in us. He is making His home in our hearts. He is our hope of glory. He is our life (Col. 3:4). To us to live is Christ.

Because He is one with us, we are different from others and different from what we were. Now we are a people filled with Christ. We are Christ-men. This is the meaning of Christian. Christians are Christ-men! We are those fully occupied by Him.

A message given by Witness Lee
in Stuttgart, Germany, April 6, 1980

© 1981 Living Stream Ministry

Published by
Living Stream Ministry
1853 W. Ball Road, Anaheim, CA 92804, U.S.A.
(714) 991-4681

THE COMPLETING MINISTRY OF PAUL

MESSAGE THREE

THE ALL-INCLUSIVE CHRIST

(1)

Scripture Reading: Rom. 1:3-4; 5:15; 8:29; 9:5; 10:12; 1 Cor. 1:30; 2:8; 3:11; 5:7; 10:4; 11:3; 12:12; 15:23, 45, 47

The second crucial point in Paul's completing ministry is the all-inclusive Christ. We shall cover this from Paul's two books, Romans and 1 Corinthians. To go through a book and see all the varied aspects of Christ presented in it will deeply impress you with His Person.

CHRIST IN ROMANS

The Designated Son of God

In Romans 1 Christ is first presented as the Son of God: "His Son, Jesus Christ our Lord, Who came out of the seed of David according to the flesh, and was designated the Son of God in power according to the Spirit of holiness out of the resurrection of the dead" (vv. 3-4).

We know that Christ is the Son of God, the Second of the Trinity. What is mentioned in these verses, however, includes His human nature as well. Because He became the descendant of David, He is no longer only divine. As the Son of God, He is God; as the Son of David, He is a man. Why did He need to be designated the Son of God? It was because He was also the Son of Man. How could a son of man be the Son of God? He had to be designated.

By what was Christ designated? His divine nature designated His human nature. Formerly, Christ was only divine. In the Second of the Trinity there was no humanity. Now, however, in Christ as the designated Son of God there is a human nature. This human nature has been designated with the divine nature.

Consider your own case. You are a son of man and also a son of God. How could you, a son of man, be a son of God? It came about by your receiving the divine nature. Now you have two natures, the human and the divine. You are one person with two natures. You are divinely human and humanly divine!

Before incarnation Christ was only divine. When He became a man, however, He took on human nature. In His divinity He was the Son of God. In His humanity, He was the Son of Man. As the Son of Man He had to be designated the Son of God, and He was so designated through resurrection. Romans 1 presents this Christ to us as the Son of God, not only divine but also human.

The Firstborn among Many Brothers

In Romans 8:29 the Son is called "the Firstborn among many brothers." We are all familiar with John 3:16, where Christ is referred to as God's "only begotten Son." What is the distinction between the Only Begotten and the Firstborn? When we believed in the Lord Jesus, we believed in Him as the only begotten Son. By believing, we became sons of God. Now that we are such, are we sons according to the Only Begotten or according to the Firstborn?

As the Only Begotten, the Son of God is unique. There could not be anyone else in His category. The Only Begotten has only the divine nature. Not until He took on human nature and was resurrected with the human nature did He become the firstborn Son. As a man in the flesh, He was begotten in resurrection to be the Son of God (Acts 13:33). When we received Him, we became sons of God according to the firstborn Son. Thus He is called the Firstborn among many brothers. We as human beings did not possess the divine nature until we received Him. Now that He has entered into us, we have received His nature in addition to the human nature we were born with.

Many of you will remember, from reading the Life-study Messages on Romans, that the goal laid out for us in the book of Romans is the producing of sons of God. Many Christians believe that the message of Romans is justification by faith. Actually, justification is simply part of the procedure by which the goal is reached. God is making sinners into His sons: this is the underlying thought in Romans.

In both the Gospel of John and the book of Romans Christ is presented to us as the Son of God. John, however, describes Him especially in His divinity, as the only begotten One, whereas Paul says in Romans that Christ is "of the seed of David according to the flesh, and was designated the Son of God in power according to the Spirit of holiness." He is speaking of Christ in the human nature being designated. In saying that Christ was of the seed of David according to the flesh, Paul is calling attention to His human nature. Then in 8:29, where Christ is called the Firstborn of many brothers, Paul is implying that it is according to Christ being the firstborn Son of God with the human nature that we are His brothers and the sons of God.

Do you believe that you also have been designated a son of God according to the Spirit of holiness? You have been! If you have faith, you will agree! Consider your family life. If you are married and have children, many times things have not gone smoothly. Your wife and your children have made things quite hard for you. Yet, just when it seemed that your wife and her little helpers would finish you off, there was a kind of designation. The power of the Spirit of holiness was with you. You did not die! You were not wiped out by your family. Instead, you were in the heavens! Possibly your in-laws were there watching what went on. They were thinking, "How could he put up with all this? Is he an angel? How could he stand so much and still be so heavenly?"

Is not such an experience a designation? If you dare not say you have been designated, you are short of faith! The divine nature is within you. You have not only a human na-

ture. You are also a son of God, not like the Only Begotten, but like the Firstborn. You were a sinner, but
Christ made you a son of God with both human and divine
natures. You are one of the many sons, and He is the Firstborn. Do you enjoy Him in this way?

Both Man and God

Romans 5:15 says, "If through the offense of the one the
many died, much more the grace of God and the gift in
grace of the One Man Jesus Christ have abounded to the
many." Here Christ is portrayed as very man. He is called
the One Man! He was a man among men. Compare this
reference with 9:5, where He is "the Christ, Who is over
all, God blessed forever." Here He is God over all. From
these two verses we can see that Christ is both man and
God.

It is in Paul's writings that we find this clear declaration that Christ is man and also God. Peter's writings do
not convey this to us as clearly. Nor does Peter tell us that
Christ lives in us. This is why Paul's ministry is the completing ministry. In this one book of Romans he says
strongly that this Christ, the very One whom we have received and are experiencing, is both man and also God
blessed forever.

Lord of All

Romans 10:12 tells us, "For there is no difference between Jew and Greek; for the same Lord of all is rich to all
who call upon Him." This Christ is Lord of all. He is over
both the Jews and the Gentiles. He is over all. He is rich to
all who call on Him.

If you will pray-read all these verses in Romans, you
will see how wonderful Christ is. He is the Son of God with
the divine nature, but also with the human nature. He is
producing many sons of God out of sinners. He is not only
God, but also man for our enjoyment. He is over all mankind. He is rich to all who call upon Him. This is the Christ
for you to call on and to enjoy! It is Paul who presents this

One in such a clear way, thus completing the divine revelation.

CHRIST IN 1 CORINTHIANS

First Corinthians is a rich book. It has much to tell us about Christ.

God's Wisdom

In 1:30 we are told that He is God's wisdom. "But of him are ye in Christ Jesus, who of God is made unto us wisdom, and righteousness, and sanctification, and redemption." This wisdom comprises three items. Christ as God's wisdom is our righteousness, our sanctification, and our redemption. Righteousness applies to our past, sanctification to our present, and redemption to our future. Christ is our righteousness for us to be justified that we might be reborn, our sanctification that we might be transformed, and our redemption that we might be transfigured. Regeneration transpires in our spirit, transformation in our soul, and transfiguration in our body. He as righteousness is for our spirit to be regenerated; as sanctification, for our soul to be transformed; and as redemption, for our body to be transfigured. Christ is our all-inclusive wisdom!

The Lord of Glory

In referring to the wisdom of God, Paul says, "Which none of the princes of this world knew: for had they known it, they would not have crucified the Lord of glory" (1 Cor. 2:8). Christ is the Lord of glory! This is a most excellent declaration. In Philippians 3 Paul says he counted all things loss on account of "the excellency of the knowledge of Christ Jesus my Lord" (v. 8). To know Christ in all these items is to have the excellency of the knowledge of Him.

What does it mean to say that Christ is the Lord of glory? This term is beyond our ability to define. To know Him as the Lord of glory is to appreciate His excellency.

The Foundation

"For other foundation can no man lay than that is laid,

which is Jesus Christ" (3:11). Christ Himself is our foundation. Upon Him alone we stand. We have no other foundation.

Our Passover

"For even Christ our passover is sacrificed for us" (5:7). For us to be redeemed, to be saved, and to be rescued from the world, Christ is our Passover. According to Exodus 12:1-13, God passed over the children of Israel because the blood of the Passover lamb had been sprinkled on the lintel and the doorposts of their houses. The children of Israel had been commanded to eat the flesh of the lamb in their houses. In other words, the house was to be their covering as they ate the lamb. As 1 Corinthians 1:30 says, it is of God that we are in Christ Jesus. He, then, is our house, our covering, as we feast upon Him as the Passover. (For a more detailed consideration of the Passover, see Exodus Life-study Messages 23, 24, and 25.)

The Rock

"And did all drink the same spiritual drink; for they drank of that spiritual Rock that followed them: and that Rock was Christ" (1 Cor. 10:4). Christ was the spiritual rock that followed God's people. Today He is the rock that follows us all the way. This rock was smitten at God's command that life might flow out to meet our need and quench our thirst (see Exo. 17:6). In the Lord's recovery this is the Christ we enjoy — the One from whom flows the water of life to quench our thirst!

The Head

"But I would have you know, that the head of every man is Christ; and the head of the woman is the man; and the head of Christ is God" (1 Cor. 11:3). Here Christ is spoken of, not as the Head of the Body, but as the head of every man. Christ is the Head!

The Body

"For as the body is one, and hath many members, and all the members of that one body, being many, are one body: so also is Christ" (12:12). He is not only the Head; He is also the Body. The whole Body is Christ. This Body comprises all of us. What this means is that Christ is all of us. How marvelous this is!

The Firstfruit

"But every man in his own order: Christ the firstfruit; afterward they that are Christ's at his coming" (15:23, lit.). Christ is the firstfruit from among the dead. He came forth from death. Since He was the first, He is the firstfruit; those that are His will follow.

The Last Adam, the Second Man

"And so it is written, The first man Adam was made a living soul; the last Adam was made a life-giving spirit. . . . The first man is of the earth, earthy: the second man is the Lord from heaven" (15:45, 47). The first man was a failure. Adam fell and missed God's purpose. With Christ, the second Man, there came in a new beginning with a new nature and a new life. He is the second, and also the last. With this last Adam there was no failure.

The Life-giving Spirit

This last Adam became a life-giving Spirit. If Christ were not the Spirit, how could He be our wisdom? our righteousness? our sanctification? our redemption? our foundation? our Passover? our rock? the Head? the Body? the firstfruit? For Christ to be all this to us, He had to become the life-giving Spirit. It is as the life-giving Spirit that He is real to us in all these different aspects.

A CLOSING WORD

Do you see how much you can learn of Christ in 1 Corinthians? Surely without this Epistle of Paul's the Bible would not be complete. You need to know this Christ. You must aspire, as Paul did, "to know Him" (Phil. 3:10). You must also experience and enjoy Him. Then you must minister to others this Christ whom you enjoy. Go out with Christ and His riches. Be filled with Him. Do not argue with people about doctrines. Preach Christ to them.

I hope you have a new appreciation of 1 Corinthians. Yes, this book does mention divisions, fornication, a law suit, and other evils. But I would rather have you focus your attention on this wonderful Christ Paul presents to us. Only in the completing ministry of Paul is Christ presented in such a rich way.

A message given by Witness Lee
in Stuttgart, Germany, April 7, 1980

Published by
Living Stream Ministry
1853 W. Ball Road, Anaheim, CA 92804, U.S.A.
(714) 991-4681

THE COMPLETING MINISTRY OF PAUL

THE ALL-INCLUSIVE CHRIST

(2)

Scripture Reading: 2 Cor. 3:17-18; 11:2; Col. 1:12, 15, 18, 19, 27; 2:2, 3, 9, 10, 16-17; 3:4, 10, 11

When I was young, I especially loved the Gospel of John because in that Gospel there are more than ten items used to describe what the Lord Jesus is. As I began to study the Epistles of Paul, however, I found many more. What Paul tells us of Christ, furthermore, is more related to life and more for our enjoyment.

Suppose in the New Testament the writings of Paul were missing. The divine revelation would not be complete. It is no wonder then, that Paul tells us he has received a commission to complete the word of God (Col. 1:25). What Paul has written is for this completing. Mainly he tells us what Christ is, not only *who* He is but especially *what* He is.

Altogether there are close to forty items in Paul's writings describing what Christ is. In our previous message we found five in Romans and fourteen in 1 Corinthians. Now we shall go on to consider those that are mentioned in 2 Corinthians and Colossians.

CHRIST IN 2 CORINTHIANS

The Spirit

In 2 Corinthians we have only two items to cover on what Christ is, but they are very meaningful. In 3:17-18 we find: "Now the Lord is the Spirit: and where the Spirit of the Lord is, there is liberty. But we all, with unveiled face beholding and reflecting as a mirror the glory of the Lord, are being transformed into the same image from glory to glory, even as from the Lord Spirit" (lit.).

Second Corinthians tells us that the Lord is the Spirit. This is a short term, the significance of which is overlooked by many Christians. They fail to realize that the ultimate expression of the Holy Spirit is the Spirit.

In Genesis 1 we have the Spirit of God brooding over the dark waters (v. 2). As the Old Testament progresses, the term Spirit of Jehovah, or Spirit of the Lord, is used. In the beginning of the New Testament we find the term Holy Spirit (Matt. 1:20). When we go on to the Lord's resurrection, we find that in resurrection the last Adam became a life-giving Spirit. This life-giving Spirit is the Spirit. The Spirit! The Spirit is the ultimate consummation of the Spirit of God, the Spirit of Jehovah, the Holy Spirit, and the Spirit of Jesus Christ (Phil. 1:19), who is the Spirit of life (Rom. 8:2) and the Spirit that gives life (John 6:63).

The title "The Spirit" is short, but its significance is profound. Its meaning is conveyed to us in typology in the compound ointment described in Exodus 30:23-33. The anointing ointment was made of olive oil compounded with four spices. At first there was only olive oil; but after it was mixed with the spices, it became a compound ointment.

Olive oil signifies the Spirit of God. The four spices — myrrh, cinnamon, calamus, and cassia — signify the death of Christ, the effectiveness of that death, His resurrection, and the power of His resurrection. The numbers mentioned all have their meaning. To add four spices to the one hin of olive oil speaks of humanity (represented by the number four) being added to divinity (the number one). A hand has five fingers: one thumb and four fingers. The number five signifies the Creator (the number one) being added to the creature (the number four). This adding of divinity to humanity is The Spirit. The Spirit comprises both God and man. Also included in The Spirit are the death of Christ, its effectiveness, His resurrection, and the power of that resurrection.

Second Corinthians 3:17 tells us that the Lord is now

the Spirit. Christ today is the ointment, the compound ointment. He is the all-inclusive, life-giving Spirit. Perhaps now you understand why we speak of the all-inclusiveness of Christ.

Our Husband

"For I am jealous over you with godly jealousy: for I have espoused you to one husband, that I may present you as a chaste virgin to Christ" (2 Cor. 11:2). It is strange that this One who in chapter three is presented as The Spirit is here called our Husband. We have a Husband.

Brothers, do you realize that we have a Husband? Do not think that only the sisters are female; spiritually speaking, we brothers are also female! In the universe there is only one Man and one woman. Christ is that Man. In fact, the German translation of this verse has "man" instead of husband. Man here actually means husband. Christ is the Man, so He is the unique Husband. Humanity is a wife. As members of the church, we are all part of the wife.

Practically speaking, how do we know Christ as the Spirit and also as our Husband? When we call on the name of the Lord, we receive the Spirit. Before He touches and captures us, we are the man. This is true even of the sisters. Some wives play the role of the husband. For a sister to lord it over her husband indicates that she is void of the Spirit. If she calls, "O Lord Jesus!" and keeps calling, the Spirit will come and touch her. He will subdue her and will Himself become the Husband!

This not only applies to the sisters. What about you brothers? I have the impression that the German men are as hard as the German bread! Who can subdue you? Nonetheless, if you will call, "O Lord Jesus!" you too will be subdued. The man, then, will be the Spirit. He will be the Husband.

When we are filled with the Spirit, we all become submissive. Christ as the Spirit is then the Husband. When Paul wrote, he was not trying to pass on a doctrine to us.

For him to say, "I have espoused you to one husband," was to say something practical. He was ministering the Spirit so that we might practically enjoy the Husband.

CHRIST IN COLOSSIANS

You may remember from the Colossians training that in this short book of only four chapters, there are fourteen different items of what Christ is. These items, I must say, are more precious to me than those in 1 Corinthians. Of course, I do appreciate those also, but the ones in Colossians are higher, richer, and more profound.

The Portion of the Saints

The Father, Colossians 1:12 tells us, has qualified us "for a share of the portion of the saints in the light." There is a portion for us. In this universe God has given us a portion or a lot. This lot is Christ, typified by the good land. When the children of Israel entered the good land, they received a lot or portion of the land. Every Israelite had his share. Our good land today is Christ. We all have a portion in this good land, promised to us by God! I trust we shall come to see what a rich portion is ours. In this portion are God, man, redemption, justification, righteousness, holiness, regeneration, and transformation. Such virtues as light, life, love, kindness, mercy, gentleness, and meekness are also in the portion. What is included in Christ as our portion is beyond enumeration. Hallelujah for such an all-inclusive portion!

The Image of God

Colossians goes on to tell us that this Christ is "the image of the invisible God" (1:15). No man has ever seen God, but Christ is His full expression. That is why He is called God's image. Image here does not mean a physical form, but an expression of God's being in all His attributes and virtues. Because Christ is God's image, when we see Him, we see God.

The Firstborn of All Creation

In this same verse, Colossians 1:15, Christ is called not only the image of the invisible God, but also the "Firstborn of all creation." How can Christ possibly be both the image of the invisible God and also the Firstborn of all creation? How can He be an item of the creation? Christ as the Firstborn of all creation is beyond the limits of our mentality. We must not restrict Him to the traditional doctrines of Christianity.

I have been accused of being a heretic for saying that Christ is a creature. My opposers insisted that Christ was the Creator and that I was in error to say He was a creature. I replied, "Was not Christ a man? Did He not become a man of flesh, blood, and bones? Is not man a creature? Do not flesh, blood, and bones pertain to the creature? Yes, Christ is the Creator, but He is also the creature. He is both God and man. As Creator, He is God; as man, He is the creature."

Christ is too great for our simplistic mentality. The more we consider all these items of what He is, the more we shall realize how far He surpasses our understanding.

Firstborn from among the Dead

Christ is not only the Firstborn of the old creation, but also the "Firstborn from among the dead" (1:18). In the old creation the first item was Christ. In the new creation, in resurrection, the first item is also Christ. Christ is the first, both in the old creation and in the new. Thus, He must have the first place in all things. The preeminence is His.

The Head of the Body

Because He is the Firstborn from among the dead, "He is the Head of the Body, the church" (v. 18). We cannot fully grasp what it means for Christ to be the Head of the church. Even our physical head the medical doctors do not fully understand. Look at me standing here. Do you see how my body supports my head? Apparently, this is the case; in actuality, it is my head that holds up my body. If you doubt my word, think what would happen if my head were cut off! Without my head, my whole body would fall. It is the head, then, which holds up the body. Without a head, we would surely be dead!

The church too has a Head! This Head is Christ. Surely we are not here supporting Him. It is not that He needs our support; rather, He is upholding us.

Strange to say, we do not realize that we enjoy Him as the Head. Day by day I enjoy the food I eat, without ever thinking of how much I appreciate my head. Yet although I could live without eating for several days, without my head I could not exist for a moment. I am alive because of my head. Similarly, the church is alive because the Head is upholding the Body.

The Beginning

He is the beginning (v. 18). This is the name by which He is twice referred to in Revelation also (21:6; 22:13). The Lord Jesus is not only the first but also the beginning. The first means that there is none before Him; the beginning, that He is the origination of all things.

These terms in Colossians are not easy to define. When the Lord Jesus says, "I am the door" (John 10:9) and "I am the good shepherd" (v. 11), we can easily grasp His meaning. But when He is called the Firstborn from among the dead, the image of God, or the Firstborn of all creation, it is hard for us to comprehend what is meant. The meaning is profound. Yet He is all of these!

The Hope of Glory

Here is another mysterious term. What does it mean for Christ in us to be "the hope of glory" (Col. 1:27)? This is far beyond our understanding. We are no longer a people without hope. We are full of hope, and this hope is Christ. We are not hoping for death or even merely for life. Our hope is of glory. This glory will be manifested to its fullest extent when Christ returns to glorify His saints (Rom.

8:30). Even now this Christ is not far from us: Christ *in you,* the hope of glory!

The Mystery of God

In Colossians 2 Paul prays that the hearts of the saints may be comforted "unto the full knowledge of the mystery of God, Christ" (v. 2). This wonderful Christ is the mystery of God. God is already a mystery. Now we have the mystery of the mystery! We cannot fathom God. And the mystery of this mysterious One is Christ. Christ is the meaning of everything in the whole universe. Behind the things for which we have no explanation is Christ. Christ is God's mystery.

A Storehouse of Wisdom and Knowledge

"In Whom are all the treasures of wisdom and knowledge hidden" (v. 3). In Christ are all the treasures of wisdom and knowledge. In this scientific age man is pursuing knowledge. We need to know that in this One who is the mystery of God are all the treasures of both wisdom and knowledge.

The Embodiment of God

Verse 9 says, "For in Him dwells all the fullness of the Godhead bodily." God is embodied in Christ. He is the totality of God. Whatever God is, has, and can do is all embodied in Christ. God is hidden in Him.

The Head

"And you in Him are made full, Who is the Head of all rule and authority" (v. 10). In our last message we saw that Christ in 1 Corinthians is the Head of every man (1 Cor. 11:3). Here He is spoken of as the Head of all rule and authority. Christ is over all earthly rulers, over all the angels, and over all other powers and authorities.

The Body of the Shadows

"Let no one therefore judge you in eating and in drinking or in respect of a feast or of a new moon or of Sabbaths, which are a shadow of things to come, but the body is of Christ" (Col. 2:16-17). From this verse we can see that all the positive things in the universe are shadows. Food, water, sunlight, Sabbaths, feasts, clothing, houses, and even transportation are all shadows. Shadows of what? They are shadows of Christ, who is the reality. Christ is our feast, our new moon, our Sabbath, our housing, and our transportation. He is our nourishment, our new beginning, our rest, our dwelling place, and our means of soaring even to the heavens! We shall be taken to the heavens in the twinkling of an eye!

Our Life

This marvelous Christ is our life (3:4).

The Constituent of the New Man

In the new man Christ is all and in all (Col. 3:10-11). Because Christ lives in us and is our life, He is the constituent of the new man. In this corporate new man there cannot be the natural person; there is only room for Christ. Even today on a small scale we can see this new man among us in the Lord's recovery. There is a new man on this earth, constituted of Christ alone!

All these descriptions of Christ are found only in Colossians. It is in this book also that Paul tells us that his ministry is to complete the word of God (1:27). How much we would lack without his writings!

A message given by Witness Lee
in Stuttgart, Germany, April 8, 1980

Published by
Living Stream Ministry
1853 W. Ball Road, Anaheim, CA 92804, U.S.A.
(714) 991-4681

THE COMPLETING MINISTRY OF PAUL

THE CHURCH

(1)

Scripture Reading: Eph. 3:2-11; 1:22-23; 4:10, 13; 2:15; 4:24; Col. 3:10-11; Eph. 5:23-27, 29-32; 2:10

Without the ministry of the Apostle Paul we would lack a clear vision not only of Christ but also of the church.

In the four Gospels the church is mentioned only twice, both times in Matthew. In chapter sixteen the Lord says that He will build His church and that the gates of Hades shall not prevail against it (v. 18). In chapter eighteen He mentions the local church (v. 17).

Acts describes the beginnings of the church and how churches were established here and there. As for a definition of the church, it is hard to come up with one based upon what we are told in the book of Acts. Our understanding of what the church is would be quite hazy if we had only the book of Acts to draw on.

The Greek word for church, *ecclesia,* means a called-out assembly or congregation. In olden times when the Greeks in a city gathered together to discuss the affairs of state, that body of citizens was called an *ecclesia.* God has called out His chosen people and gathered them together: this is the church. Just by understanding the meaning of the word, however, we do not know much about the church.

Paul's writings are where we find the church presented in the clearest, most thorough way. In this message we shall cover six ways in which Paul describes the church; then in the next message we shall go over another six. All twelve are profound and rich in meaning.

I. THE MYSTERY OF CHRIST

In Ephesians 3:4 the church is called the mystery of Christ.

We saw in our previous message that Christ is the mystery of God (Col. 2:2). No human mentality can understand God, yet Christ fully defines Him. Christ is also His embodiment and expression. We may say that Christ is the story of God. The story of God is the same as the mystery of God.

Just as Christ is the mystery of God, so the church is the mystery of Christ. Christ Himself is a mystery. Through all these twenty centuries no one has come on the scene who can compare with Him. His name has spread throughout the earth. Surely He must be powerful and wise. Yet who can understand Him? He is a mystery. All these years very few have realized who He is. Paul was among these few. Nonetheless, this mystery has a definition, and this definition is the church. The church is the story of Christ. It is His embodiment. To see Christ we must come to the church. Where is God? He is in Christ. Where is Christ? He is in the church. Whoever wants to see God must contact Christ. Whoever would see Christ must come to the church.

Even as we meet here for this training, we are the mystery of Christ! Apparently we are a gathering of people from many different countries. We have here Germans, French, Italians, Spaniards, Norwegians, Danes, Swedes, Dutch, British, Americans, and Orientals. In actuality, however, we are not gathered here as an assortment of different nationalities. We are all part of Christ. We are not like the United Nations! The church is Christ. We are here as Christ. Our nationality is buried. What we are is buried. All that is left in the church is Christ.

As Ephesians 3:2-11 makes clear, the mystery of Christ implies His unsearchable riches. All these riches are found in the church. The church is not the place for American philosophy, Chinese ethics, or German scientific research. There is room only for Christ and His unsearchable riches. Thus, through the church the multifarious wisdom of God is being made known to the rulers and the authorities in the heavenlies. All this is according to God's eternal purpose, which He purposed in Christ.

What we are touching here is profoundly great. It is outside the realm of philosophy, religion, or science. This mystery is nothing less than Christ with all His unsearchable riches. I hope you will go over these verses and pray-read them. You need to realize what they say not by your mental ability but by revelation. This revelation comes to your spirit, not to your mind. If you exercise your spirit and pray over these verses, you will see this mystery: the mystery of Christ, which is the church, containing His unsearchable riches and making known God's wisdom according to His eternal purpose.

II. THE BODY OF CHRIST

The church is also His Body (Eph. 1:22-23). Only in Paul's writings do we find the church described as the Body of Christ. This term is not found in the Gospels nor in Acts.

The human body is a marvel. Medical students spend years learning how it is put together. After such a comprehensive study, they surely must admit that some mighty Being is behind this universe. There can be no other reasonable explanation for all its intricacies.

The church is even more wonderful. It is a Body for Christ. Christ has a Body. Some Bible teachers think that the Body of Christ is a metaphor, a figure of speech, to help us understand what the church is. I used to teach that myself. The more I studied the Bible, however, the more I realized that the Body of Christ is not a mere figure of speech. It is a fact and a reality.

A body is a living organism. It is not like this stand, which was made of pieces of wood put together in a certain way. A body is not made by attaching bones together; that result would be a lifeless skeleton. Every part of the human body is organic; it has life. Our teeth are organic; only false teeth have no life. Our ears are organic. I knew a brother who had a false ear; he could take it off. His own ear had been removed because of cancer. That prosthetic ear was not organic. My glasses are not organic. They are replacing the lenses that were removed from my eyes when I had surgery for cataracts. Those original lenses in my eyes were organic; these that I wear now have no life whatever.

There is deep significance in the church as the organic Body of Christ. In Christianity today there are many false teeth, false limbs, and mechanical motions! The impression is that of a robot, made of wood or steel. When a living person stands, or raises his arm, or bends, all his actions stem from life. He is not a mechanical device put together to seem human. He is living! So is the church! It is Christ's Body to express Him in a living way. There is no need to perform. This organism is the way it is because of life. The way the brothers and sisters are should be the result of life, not of a performance. The Body of Christ is His expression.

Notice from these verses (Eph. 1:22-23) that Christ has been made "Head over all things to the church, which is His Body." The church is one with Christ, sharing and enjoying His headship. He has been made Head over all, and as His Body we are one with Him, enjoying His headship.

III. THE FULLNESS

The church is also "the fullness of the One Who fills all in all" (v. 23). This is hard to explain. Suppose we compare two brothers. One is much heavier than the other. The heavier one is fuller than the smaller one. The church is the fullness of Christ (4:13). Because this Christ is so vast that He fills all in all, He needs a great, universal Body. This Body is His fullness, the fullness of the One who fills all in all. Consider how great the Body of Christ is. It is spread throughout the earth. It can be found in Europe, in North America, in the Far East, in Australasia, in Africa, and in South America. How vast is this Body!

In 1958 I was staying in London, England. One day a

brother there took me to a huge greenhouse to show me the queen's grapevine. That vine filled the whole greenhouse. "Brother Lee," the brother asked, "have you ever seen such a great grapevine?" He was proud of that vine belonging to the British queen.

"Yes," I replied, "I have seen a far greater one than this!" I reminded him of the vine in John 15, where the Lord Jesus said He was the true vine and the believers were the branches.

Can you tell me how great this vine is? The queen's vine is insignificant compared to it. The vine in John 15 is universally great. The whole universe is its greenhouse. What fullness!

When the Lord Jesus was on earth, He was in only one place at a time. If He was in Samaria, He was not in Galilee. When He was in Bethlehem, He was not in Jerusalem. He was limited in time and in space. After His resurrection, however, all the limitations were done away. Now Christ is the vine which has spread to every corner of the earth. Even while He is here in Germany, He is also in Japan and Africa and everywhere else.

What is the fullness of Christ? It is the church. Sometimes someone will ask me, "Where is your church?" It is hard for me to answer! I want to say that my church is universally great. Does that sound like boasting? Do you realize how great the church is to us in the recovery? This church began in Acts 2 on the day of Pentecost and is now spreading throughout the whole earth. This church is the fullness of the One who fills all things (Eph. 4:10).

IV. THE NEW MAN

The church is also the new man (Eph. 2:15; 4:24; Col. 3:10). There is a sense in which the whole human race is just one man. All the different peoples on earth comprise this one man, who in the Scripture is called the old man or Adam. God at the beginning did not create two men, but only Adam. This one man was mankind. In Genesis 1:26-27 the whole human race was created.

But on the cross, through Christ and in Him, God created another man, a new man! This man is also corporate; we are included in him. Adam was the old man; Christ with the church is the new man. This new man is not only Christ, but also the church. Christ is the Head of this universal man; the church is His Body.

As the body exists for the expression of the head, so the church as the Body of Christ is Christ's expression. As man exists for the expression of God, so the church as the new man is God's expression. The whole church is a corporate yet single man. There are many local churches all over Europe, yet altogether they are only one man. Throughout the earth today, this one universal man expresses God. As the Body, the church expresses Christ. As the new man, the church expresses God.

The modern conveniences available to us in the second half of the twentieth century have greatly facilitated the spread of the recovery. Saints from many nationalities can come together, correspond, and even converse by phone. Just recently in one afternoon I received phone calls from Hong Kong, Taiwan, and Texas, all within the space of about twenty minutes. What a help these conveniences are for the new man! Even the messages given here are videotaped and can then be quickly sent out to all five continents; soon they will be seen in South America, Africa, Australasia, the Far East, and North America. Even one hundred years ago it took six months for a missionary to travel from the United States to China; some of them died soon after they arrived. Nowadays it is possible to be in Peking, China, within twenty-four hours and then to be back home within another twenty-four hours. How we praise the Lord for His sovereign rulership! He has arranged all these things for the good of the new man!

V. THE BRIDE OF CHRIST

How wonderful that the church is a man and, at the same time, a bride (Eph. 5:23-27, 29-32)! Are we male or female?

For expressing God, we must be male. Sisters, I want to speak to you about your tears. As members of the new man, do not consider yourself female. Do not shed tears! They are a sign of the weaker vessel. In all these twenty or so years since I came to the western world for the ministry, I have never shed a tear. This is because I am a man. Sisters, you must no longer be characterized by tears! You are members of the new man. From now on, no more tears!

When it comes to loving Christ, however, the church is the bride. In this sense, all the brothers are also female and should not act as men. Day by day we are the bride, loving Christ.

Here, then, is our twofold role. As the man, we daily tell God, "Father, we are the man, expressing You on the earth." As the bride, we then turn to the Lord Jesus and say, "Lord, we want You to know that we love You. We are Your bride." The man's position is a matter of expression. The woman's is a matter of love.

If you consider the first couple, you will remember that God did not create Eve. Eve was made from a rib of Adam. God built a wife for Adam from that bone. She was part of him. The church is likewise part of Christ. The two are one in nature, in life, and in existence. The church is not independent. Eve came from Adam and went back to him; they two became one flesh (Gen. 2:21-24). The church and Christ are one spirit. The church came out from Christ and goes back to Him. This relationship is one of love. Love issues in genuine oneness. If two cannot be one, it is due to a lack of love. The church and Christ are genuinely one, one spirit. This oneness is the expression of their love. The church, then, is Christ's loving bride.

VI. GOD'S MASTERPIECE

Ephesians 2:10 says, "For we are His workmanship." The Greek word for workmanship, *poiema*, can also be translated masterpiece or poem. It conveys the thought of a piece of work that expresses its maker or author. The church is a poem! In the whole universe the church stands out as an expression of God's wisdom; its design cannot be improved upon. It is like pleasant music or a lovely poem. What a matchless display of divine wisdom! Who can improve on this supreme handiwork of God!

When it comes to the way a building is designed, there can always be changes and improvements made. An architect often modifies his designs, as he becomes aware of their shortcomings. But what God designs has no room for improvement. Man cannot imitate it. Any adjustment would be for the worse. Consider the way the human body was designed. What a work of art the facial pattern alone is! The placement of our two eyes, our two ears, our nose, and our lips makes a beautiful appearance. Our body with two shoulders, two lovely hands, and so forth, is worthy of admiration. The church is a far greater, more magnificent design than the human body! The church is a poem declaring and demonstrating God's wisdom and design.

A SUMMARY

Through Paul's writings we know that the church is the mystery of Christ, the Body of Christ, the fullness of the One who fills all in all, the new man expressing God, the bride of Christ loving Him and being one with Him, and a poem expressing God's wisdom and God's design. How rich is our understanding of the church because of Paul's completing ministry!

A message given by Witness Lee
in Stuttgart, Germany, April 9, 1980

© 1981 Living Stream Ministry

Published by
Living Stream Ministry
1853 W. Ball Road, Anaheim, CA 92804, U.S.A.
(714) 991-4681

THE COMPLETING MINISTRY OF PAUL

MESSAGE SIX

THE CHURCH

(2)

Scripture Reading: Eph. 2:19-22; 6:11-18; Gal. 6:10, 16

Many Christians consider the church as merely the gathering of God's called-out ones. This is correct, but it does not touch the significance of the church. Actually, the church is Christ's continuation, reproduction, multiplication, and spread. The New Testament — in Paul's writings, which conclude the divine revelation — tells us that Christ is the mystery of God and that the church is the mystery of Christ. To call Christ the mystery of God is to imply that He is one with God, that He is God expressed, that He is God's story. In the same principle the church as the mystery of Christ is Christ's expression and His story.

We may say that the church is Christ. To the ears of those who lack a clear vision such a statement sounds blasphemous. To them the church is made up of human beings who have been called together as a congregation. In their thinking, to say that the church is Christ or His continuation is to deify it. No, the church is not God, but it does have the divine nature.

Consider how the church is described in Paul's writings. Nearly every item implies an organic relationship. The church has been born of God in Christ. It has received His life and nature, no less than a child has his father's life and nature. To say that a child is the same as his father in life and nature is not objectionable. But this is also true of the church. The church, however, is not deified. It is not an object of worship. Only God is to be worshipped.

The church is the Body of Christ. Surely the human

body has the same life and nature as the head. In life and nature the church is one with Christ. Yet Christ is the Lord; the church is not. Christ as Lord is worthy of worship, but we are not to worship the church.

The church is the bride of Christ. As Eve was formed from Adam's rib, so the church came out of Christ. The rib signifies eternal life. The church is produced from the divine life. Then Eve returned to Adam and became one flesh with him. Similarly, the church has returned to Christ and is now one spirit with Him. Here again, the picture is of an organic relationship. We are organically one with Christ. He expresses God; we express Him.

In the previous message we went over six descriptions Paul gives of the church. Now we shall go on to another six descriptions of what the church is.

VII. THE HOUSEHOLD OF GOD

"You are . . . members of the household of God," Paul tells us in Ephesians 2:19. The Greek word for household means family and house. In our thinking, a house is one thing and a family another. A house is the building where we live, and a family consists of parents and children. We have a house in which we live and a family with whom we live. In the New Testament sense, however, the house and the family are the same. God's house is His family. We are both His house and His family — His household. God has only His family as His house. He lives in us and considers us His house.

Household is another term implying an organic relationship. We are no longer "strangers and sojourners" but organically God's family. We are God's folks! We were born of God and now have His life and nature. This is not true of the angels. You may wish you were an angel and try to act angelic, but the angels are not God's children. They are His servants; because they are our Father's servants, they are our servants also. We are better than servants! We are God's family.

VIII. THE KINGDOM OF GOD

Besides being members of the household of God, we are also called fellow-citizens of the saints (Eph. 2:19). This term indicates the kingdom of God. Household refers to a life relationship, whereas kingdom refers to authority. The church has not only God's life, but also His authority. God is both the Father and the King. We are therefore members of a royal family! As those who were born into God's household, we have His life and enjoy His riches. As fellow-citizens in His kingdom, we are under His authority and have His authority. God's kingdom is the realm where He exercises this authority. We are the King's citizens!

IX. GOD'S DWELLING PLACE

This household of God is "being built upon the foundation of the apostles and prophets, Christ Jesus Himself being the cornerstone, in Whom all the building, being fitted together, is growing into a holy temple in the Lord, in Whom you also are being built together into a dwelling place of God in spirit" (Eph. 2:20-22).

The Need for Building Up

From these verses we can see that the household of God needs to be built up. God's family or household needs to be built together. A pile of lumber or stones is not a house. For a house to be built, every piece of material must be strictly used. Even though we are God's family, for us to become His dwelling place we must be built up. This building up is not mentioned in verse 19, but in the next three verses, quoted above. First the universal building is referred to and then the local. We need this twofold building: with the saints in our locality and with all the saints on earth.

Verse 20 gives us a general description of the building upon the foundation of the apostles and prophets, with Christ Jesus as the cornerstone. Then verse 21 describes the universal building: "In whom all the building, being fitted together, is growing into a holy temple in the Lord." All the saints on earth are to be built up into a holy temple.

This temple is the universal church, after it has been built up. In verse 22 "you also" indicates that the local saints are referred to. Not only are all the believers throughout the world to be built up; "you also are being built together into a dwelling place of God in spirit."

In our consideration of the church, we need to pay attention to this matter of building. Are we God's family? We have no hesitation in replying, "Praise the Lord, we are!" But here is another question: Are we, practically speaking, the dwelling place of God? This one we cannot answer so quickly.

To be God's family is not a matter of building. But for God to have a dwelling place requires building up. If we are scattered around, as is the case with most Christians, there is surely no building. Praise the Lord that we have been brought into His recovery! We are no longer scattered. Now we are meeting together. Does this mean that we have been built up? Not necessarily. After we have met together for a while, we may feel that we know each other and have some affection toward one another. This, again, is not necessarily the building. It is more like a pile. The building materials have been brought together and piled up. Surely a pile is not a dwelling place!

As we meet together, are we a pile or a building? A building must have all its pieces properly trimmed and fitted together. Each piece must be put in place in proper relationship to the other pieces. When all the pieces have been dealt with and have grown up in relation to each other so that they are fitted together, there is the building. Meeting together might be just a piling up; only building up provides a dwelling place.

As God's family, we should be His house. A family, however, is a matter of life by birth, while a dwelling place includes not only life but also building. When there is both building and life, there is the dwelling place.

On this earth our God is nearly homeless. He has a family, but He has no house to live in. We are all God's family as we meet here. In a sense, we are having a family reunion. A family may be scattered over many different countries, but on special occasions they all come together for a happy reunion. This reunion, however, is not a home. For a home there must be a building. God has a big family on this earth. Wherever we go, we can meet some of His children. Nonetheless, He has no home because there is no building.

The believers possessing His life are many, but they have not been built up. Those of you who are here from Blackpool must have the assurance that in Blackpool there is not only God's family but also His dwelling place. There must be the building as well as the life. To be God's family it is sufficient to have God's life; for God to have a home, however, you must all be built together. The same is true of Stuttgart. I hope that you have here not only life but also building. What about those of you from Denmark? from Neuchatel? from other localities? You have the family; do you also have the dwelling place?

Local and Universal

This building is twofold. It has a local aspect and a universal aspect. Locally, we are God's dwelling place; universally, the Lord's holy temple. For example, as a member of the church in Anaheim, I have been built up with the saints there. More than this, however, I do believe that I have also been built up with all the saints on this earth. Thus I have a twofold building, both local and universal, wherever there are churches. While I am here in Stuttgart, I do not consider myself a stranger or sojourner; I am a part of the universal holy temple in the Lord.

How to Be Built Up

To be built up does not mean that you are close to each other. Two pieces of lumber may be right next to each other and still not be part of the building. You may be close together without being built up. Formerly I would tell the saints that they needed to know who was beside them, and above them, and behind them, and beneath them, and in front of them. To be built up, I taught, was to know where you fit in the house, like pieces of wood fitted into a building. I realize now that this explanation is a human concept.

To be built up is to grow together. Ephesians 4 explains this: "But holding to truth in love, we may grow up into Him in all things, Who is the Head, Christ, out from Whom all the Body, fitted and knit together . . . causes the growth of the Body unto the building up of itself in love" (vv. 15-16). The real building is a growing. To grow up is to get out of yourself and to grow into Christ the Head. This happens gradually. How much you get out of yourself and into the Head is the deciding factor in your growth. It is also the deciding factor in your being built up. When you get out of yourself and grow into Christ, you are built up.

Here again I would call to your attention that it is Paul in his completing ministry who deals with our being built up. It is from his writings that we can see that we are God's family, but that whether we are God's dwelling place depends on our being built up; that the building up depends upon the growing up; and that the more we grow into Christ and are built up, the more dwelling place God has.

X. THE WARRIOR

From the exhortations in Ephesians 6:11-18 we can see that the church is also a warrior, needing the whole armor of God to stand against the stratagems of the Devil.

In this universe a war is raging. The church must be a fighter, battling for God's kingdom and against God's enemy. The church is not only a man, a bride, God's family, and His dwelling place. It is also a warrior, equipped by God to do battle against Satan and the powers of darkness under him. The troubles that happen on this earth come mainly from these evil, spiritual powers in the air. It is the church which must stand against these evil powers of darkness.

This warfare is waged not in the church's own strength

but in Christ. He Himself is the armor provided by God for us. It is up to us, however, to take up and put on the armor. Christ is the girdle for our loins, the shield to quench Satan's flaming darts, the helmet of salvation, and the sword to slay the foe. We put on Christ, wearing Him like a garment and hiding in Him, to fight the battle for God.

XI. THE HOUSEHOLD OF THE FAITH

The ten descriptions of the church that we have already considered — the mystery of Christ, His Body, His fullness, the new man, His bride, God's masterpiece, God's family, the kingdom of God, God's dwelling place, and the warrior — are all found in Ephesians. For the last two descriptions we turn now to Galatians.

In Galatians 6:10 the church is called the household of the faith. In Paul's completing ministry here is yet another revelation of what the church is. The household of *the* faith is a specific term; it means the family of the faith.

In Galatians Paul sets the law and faith in contrast. The Judaizers are people of the law, while the believers are the family of the faith. One belongs to the Old Testament, the other to the New. This term, the faith, indicates God's New Testament economy. It is a comprehensive way of saying that what God is doing now is nothing less than dispensing Himself into His chosen people. We may say that faith is a bundle, wrapping up God's New Testament economy.

This faith comes into us by our knowing and appreciating Christ. As we hear of Him, we begin to know Him and, correspondingly, to appreciate Him. Out of this appreciation, faith is produced within us. We thus receive Christ and have the Triune God dispensed into our being. All of this thought is included in "the faith." We belong to this faith, not to the law. The law cannot give life; thus, it has no family. The people of the law are without life. The faith, in contrast, imparts life, even God Himself, into us. Thus, faith has a family.

We believers are the household of the begetting faith!

We are the members of a family that is spread throughout the earth. This family has a name: the household of the faith. We are members of this great family of the faith — the church!

XII. THE ISRAEL OF GOD

In the Old Testament God had a people to be His testimony, expressing Him. This was the nation of Israel. In the New Testament the real Israel of God is the church. "Israel of God" is the term Paul uses in Galatians 6:16.

There is today the nation of Israel. This is Israel in the flesh. It is not the real Israel. The real Israel of God today is the church. Thus there are two Israels: the one in the flesh, located in what was called Palestine, and the one in the Spirit, to which we belong. Paul tells us that as many as walk according to the rule of the new creation are the Israel of God.

Have you ever considered that you are a real Jew? If you do not realize this, you are not familiar enough with the completing ministry of Paul. Because of Galatians 6:16 I dare to say that I am a real Jew! The Jews in the land of Israel are not the real Jews. If you visit there, you will find that they do not express God at all; the situation is worldly and even sinful. That was my impression when I stayed there for some days a few years ago. Nonetheless, they are still the Israel of God, but in the flesh. We are the Israel of God in Spirit. All the blessings promised by God in the Bible are our portion because we are the church.

This wonderful church is revealed to us in Paul's writings. He has surely completed the Word of God (Col. 1:25).

A message given by Witness Lee
in Stuttgart, Germany, April 10, 1980

Published by
Living Stream Ministry
1853 W. Ball Road, Anaheim, CA 92804, U.S.A.
(714) 991-4681

THE COMPLETING MINISTRY OF PAUL

MESSAGE SEVEN

THE SPIRIT AND OUR SPIRIT

Scripture Reading: Rom. 8:9; Luke 1:35; Acts 16:7; Phil. 1:19; 2 Cor. 3:17-18; Rom. 8:2; 1 Cor. 15:45b; John 7:39; Gal. 3:14; John 3:6b; Rom. 8:16; 1 Cor. 6:17; Rom. 8:6b, 4

Without the Spirit in our spirit all the matters we have covered about Christ living in us, about His being so many different items for our enjoyment, and about what the church is, cannot be prevailing.

How can Christ live in us? It is by His being the Spirit in our spirit. It is the Spirit that lives in our spirit. How can Christ be enjoyed by us in the many different aspects we have mentioned? If He were not the life-giving Spirit, all that He is would be objective and remote. Because He is the Spirit, whatever He is we may enjoy in our spirit. How can the church be the mystery of Christ, the Body of Christ, and the new man? Again, it is by the Spirit in our spirit.

Only by the Spirit in our spirit will all the crucial points in Paul's completing ministry become prevailing. Again and again Paul refers us to the Spirit and to our spirit. His writings thoroughly cover these two spirits.

THE PROGRESSIVE REVELATION OF THE SPIRIT OF GOD

The Old Testament mostly uses the term "Spirit of God," as in Genesis 1:2. Further on in the Old Testament we find the term "Spirit of Jehovah" (e.g., Judg. 6:34). At the end of the Old Testament there is even the remarkable term "Spirit of grace" (Zech. 12:10). Spirit of holiness is also mentioned (Isa. 63:10, 11; Psa. 51:11; lit.). "Spirit of God" and "Spirit of Jehovah," however, are the two commonly used Old Testament terms.

In the New Testament mostly the terms Holy Spirit, Spirit of God, and the Spirit are used. Paul uses many other terms as well. "Spirit of God" is found in his writings (Rom. 8:9), but now He is no longer brooding over the waters; He "dwells in you." The brooding Spirit today is indwelling us. What a change from Genesis 1!

The Holy Spirit

Paul also uses the term Holy Spirit a number of times in his Epistles.

Luke 1:35 gives us the first mention of the Holy Spirit. He is introduced at the time when the Lord Jesus was conceived by a human mother. This is because something common is to be made holy. In this same verse the One to be born is called "that holy thing." The Holy Spirit came into a human being to conceive something holy. When the Holy Spirit came into us common human beings, we too could be made holy.

The Spirit of Jesus

In Acts 16:7 (lit.) it says, "The Spirit of Jesus suffered them not." This term is found only in this verse. It indicates that when the Lord Jesus was walking on this earth, the Spirit of God was with Him. Jesus was a man, yet the Spirit of God was with Him. This Spirit became the Spirit of Jesus to live a human life.

The Spirit of Christ

Romans 8:9 has the term Spirit of Christ. While the Spirit of Jesus relates to human living, the Spirit of Christ relates to resurrection life. On earth the Lord Jesus lived a human life by the Spirit of Jesus. Now that He has entered into resurrection, He lives a resurrected life by the Spirit of Christ.

The Spirit of Jesus Christ

Philippians 1:19 has the expression "the Spirit of Jesus Christ." This is the all-inclusive, compound Spirit. Do not think that there are several different Spirits, all with different names: the Spirit of God, the Holy Spirit, the Spirit of Jesus, the Spirit of Christ, and now the Spirit of Jesus Christ. There is only one Spirit. His different names indicate different aspects of this all-inclusive Spirit.

When He is called the Spirit of Jesus Christ, this name includes the Spirit of God, the Holy Spirit, the Spirit of Jesus, and the Spirit of Christ. In the Spirit of God there was only divinity, but now the Spirit of Jesus Christ includes humanity also. In addition, His human living, His death, and His resurrection are included.

Again I refer you to the anointing ointment in Exodus 30. The oil alone speaks of the Spirit of God, or divinity. But four spices were to be added to the olive oil and compounded with it to make an ointment. With these ingredients added, the oil was no longer a single element.

To the oil was added myrrh, which speaks of Christ's death; cinnamon, signifying the effectiveness of His death; calamus, which typifies His resurrection; and cassia, representing the power of His resurrection. These four spices plus the one hin of olive oil tell us that God (represented by the number one) is joined to man (represented by the number four); that is, divinity is added to humanity.

The amount of spices used in the ointment is also meaningful:

(1) Myrrh - 500 shekels (v. 23)
(2) Cinnamon - 250 shekels (v. 23)
(3) Calamus - 250 shekels (v. 23)
(4) Cassia - 500 shekels (v. 24).

These four spices are of three units of five hundred. Three speaks of the Triune God. Why is the second unit of five hundred shekels divided between the cinnamon and the calamus? This is an indication that the second of the Godhead was split on the cross.

From this Old Testament picture we learn that in the Spirit of Jesus Christ, this compounded Spirit, there is divinity, humanity, human living, the death of Christ — even the cutting on the cross — and its effectiveness, the resurrection of Christ and its power. Surely this compound, all-inclusive Spirit has a bountiful supply!

His resources, which are with us and available to us as a bountiful supply, include divinity; a proper, uplifted humanity; the proper human living; Christ's wonderful death and its effectiveness; His resurrection and its power, especially its repelling power.

This all-inclusive Spirit with such a bountiful supply is with us!

The Spirit of the Lord

"Now the Lord is the Spirit: and where the Spirit of the Lord is, there is liberty. But we all, with unveiled face beholding and reflecting as a mirror the glory of the Lord, are being transformed into the same image from glory to glory, even as from the Lord Spirit" (2 Cor. 3:17-18, lit.). These verses are puzzling in their reference to the Spirit. First we are told that the Lord is the Spirit. This means that the Lord and the Spirit are one. Then in the same verse we have the Spirit of the Lord. This term sounds as if the Spirit is related to the Lord, but that the Spirit is one Person and the Lord another. Then in verse 18 we have the term Lord Spirit. This is a compound title like Father God. When we say Father God, we do not mean that Father is one and God another. The same is true with "Lord Spirit"; Lord and Spirit are one.

Electricity illustrates this thought. When electricity moves, it is called electric current. The current, however, is not one thing and electricity another. The current is simply electricity in motion. Similarly, the Lord is the Lord; when He moves, He is the Spirit, or the Spirit of the Lord. While the Lord is in the heavens, He is the Lord. When He comes to us, He is the Spirit. The Spirit of the Lord is the Lord moving in us. We can say this from experience, not merely as a doctrine. Many men of God throughout the centuries have spoken this way also. When God or Christ comes to us, it is as the Spirit that He comes.

Who is it that lives in us? It is the Spirit. Who is the

Spirit? He is the Lord. He is also the Father. According to the New Testament, the Father, the Son, and the Spirit are all in us. Do we have three Persons within? We cannot answer too hastily. Ephesians 4:6 says that the Father is in us. Colossians 1:27 says that Christ is in us. Romans 8:9 tells us that the Spirit of God dwells in us. How many are in us? This is a mystery. When we have the Spirit, we have the Son. When we have the Son, we have the Father. With the Spirit we have both the Father and the Son. When we have one, we have all three! They cannot be separated. The Spirit of the Lord is a wonderful Spirit!

The Spirit of Life

The Spirit of life is mentioned in Romans 8:2. This term is not easy to define. Life itself cannot easily be defined in words, but it is easily identified. When you look at someone, you can tell immediately that he is alive. If you go to a mortuary, it is plain to see that a dead person has no life. You do not need to declare that you are living or try to persuade others that you have life. They can tell even without a glance that you are alive. By the same token, it is immediately apparent when someone is dead: the life has gone.

When you have the Spirit of life, you are living. You show signs of life! This indicates that you have God and Christ, who are life. The Spirit is the Spirit of life.

The Life-giving Spirit

"The last Adam became a life-giving Spirit" (1 Cor. 15:45b). This Spirit is not only the Spirit of life; He is also the One who imparts life. He is life-giving!

The Spirit

This is a short term, but it is the greatest one! "This He said concerning the Spirit, Whom those who believed in Him were about to receive; for the Spirit was not yet, because Jesus was not yet glorified" (John 7:39).

How strange to say "the Spirit was not yet"! The Spirit

of God had already been mentioned in both the Old and New Testaments many times. What is meant by the Spirit? Because Jesus had yet to pass through death and resurrection and be glorified, the Spirit of Jesus Christ — the all-inclusive, compound, life-giving Spirit — was not yet. Today we have this Spirit! We have received the promise of the Spirit through faith (Gal. 3:14).

OUR SPIRIT

Born of the Spirit

Physically we were born of our parents, but, when we were regenerated, we were "born of the Spirit" (John 3:6). By believing in the Lord Jesus, our spirit was born of the Spirit. The all-inclusive Spirit came into our spirit to regenerate it with the divine life.

The Spirit with Our Spirit

"The Spirit Himself witnesses with our spirit that we are the children of God" (Rom. 8:16). Now that the Spirit is within our spirit through regeneration, He witnesses with our spirit, testifying that we are the children of God. These two spirits within us correspond to each other, together confirming that we are God's children.

One Spirit with the Lord

The Spirit today is the Triune God with human nature, human living, Christ's all-inclusive death, and also His resurrection. First Corinthians 6:17 says, "He that is joined unto the Lord is one spirit." Our spirit is mingled as one with this Spirit.

Your aspiration may be to walk in the presence of God. You may have read Brother Lawrence's booklet, "The Practice of the Presence of God." Do you realize that to be in God's presence is an Old Testament concept? Abraham walked in God's presence. However close to God you walk, however much you fear Him and seek to please Him, you and He are still separate from each other. The New Testament does not exhort us to practice God's presence. It says,

"He that is joined unto the Lord is one spirit!" We are one spirit with the Lord. Abraham did not experience this. God was not in Abraham, nor was Abraham in God. At best, Abraham could walk in His presence.

We are one spirit with God! What a tremendous difference from merely being in His presence! Not only are we one with God; we are also one spirit with Him. The day I saw this I was thrilled beyond words. From that time on, I began to practice being one spirit with Him. I failed again and again. I behaved well. I did not lose my temper. My conduct was above reproach. Nonetheless, the good things I did were apart from God. Being close to Him or walking in His presence is not the same as being one spirit with Him. I loved the Bible. I loved the church. I was humble in my manner and kind in my relationships with others. Nonetheless, at the end of the day, I would find myself confessing my failure. "Lord, forgive me. This whole day has been a failure. I loved the saints, but I did so apart from You. I did many kind deeds, but I did them apart from You. I did not live one spirit with You. I was practicing Christian ethics. I did not practice being one spirit with You. Forgive me, Lord. Wash me."

How well I know now that it is not easy to practice being one spirit with the Lord! For over fifty years I have been practicing good behavior, spiritual ethics. It is easy to control my temper. It is easy to be humble. It is easy to treat people pleasantly. For all these years I have been building up these habits. Why do I need the Lord? He can stay away, while I live my highly moral life from morning till evening. It is spontaneous and natural for me to live in such a virtuous way.

When it comes to practicing one spirit with the Lord, however, the only time I succeed is when I am in prayer. When the prayer is over, I slip away. Since I saw that we are one spirit with the Lord, I have been exercising to stay with Him. I dare not leave Him. I must remain in Him, constantly praying. He says, "Abide in Me and I in you. . . . I am the vine, you are the branches" (John 15:4-5). This mutual abiding is not the practice of His presence. It is rather the practice of being one spirit with Him.

The Mind Set on the Spirit

"The mind set on the spirit is life and peace" (Rom. 8:6). All day long we must set our mind on this mingled spirit.

Walking according to Spirit

To walk according to spirit (Rom. 8:4) is to practice being one spirit with Him. We must set our mind on and walk according to this one spirit, our spirit mingled with His. "Lord," we can tell Him, "I don't care whether I love others or hate them. It doesn't matter whether I am proud or humble. These things no longer concern me. All I want to do is to set my mind on the spirit and walk according to the spirit. I want to practice this spiritual fact: that I am one spirit with You."

To practice being one spirit with the Lord is the consummate point of Paul's completing ministry. Do not try to overcome sin or the world. Do not try to be spiritual. Simply set your mind on the spirit, and walk according to this one spirit.

A message given by Witness Lee
in Stuttgart, Germany, April 11, 1980

Published by
Living Stream Ministry
1853 W. Ball Road, Anaheim, CA 92804, U.S.A.
(714) 991-4681

THE COMPLETING MINISTRY OF PAUL

MESSAGE EIGHT

TRANSFORMATION FOR GOD'S BUILDING

Scripture Reading: Rom. 12:2; 2 Cor. 3:17-18

It is clearly revealed in the Bible that God's intention is to work Himself into man so that He can be man's life and that man may be His expression. It was for this very purpose that God created man in His own image; man thus had the possibility of expressing God. Man was also created with a spirit; this was so that he might be able to receive God the Spirit into him. As we know, man fell.

Then God came in the Son as a man. He lived on the earth for thirty-three and a half years. At the end of His human living, He went to the cross and died there for man's sin. Through that death He also destroyed Satan and terminated the old creation. After three days in the tomb, He entered into resurrection. When He was resurrected, He brought humanity into divinity, thus uplifting fallen humanity. This uplifted humanity is now in Him in resurrection. At this same time He became the life-giving Spirit, able and ready to enter whoever believes in Him.

Whenever and wherever a person believes in the Lord Jesus, this life-giving Spirit comes into him and regenerates his spirit. The divine Spirit then indwells that believer's spirit and becomes one with it. He is saved, redeemed, regenerated. He possesses God's life and nature. He is joined to the Lord and is one spirit with Him (1 Cor. 6:17). Now all he needs to do is to live Christ, to live one spirit with the Lord.

GOD REPLACED

When man fell, he lost God. Because he had fallen away from God, certain things came in to replace God. Eventually in the fallen man God was replaced by the following things.

The Knowledge of Good and Evil

The knowledge of good and evil came in. Man began to know the difference between good and evil. He tried to do the good and forsake the evil. Whether he could succeed was another matter, but he did gain this knowledge and attempt to choose the good and reject the evil.

Culture

Culture is a development of the knowledge of good and evil. We can say there are many different cultures, like Egyptian, Babylonian, Jewish, Greek, Roman, European, American, Chinese, Japanese, and Indian. Nonetheless, all these cultures promote the good and denounce the evil. Human beings of every race and culture like to do good and turn away from evil. This is what their culture teaches them.

Philosophy

Philosophy is a further development of culture. It is a higher stage, but its principle is the same as that of culture. It extols good and condemns evil.

Ethics

Ethics promote morality. Among the various ethical teachings man has produced, those of Confucius rank the highest. Ethics encourage man to live according to certain principles of conduct. These principles are also based upon the knowledge of good and evil.

Religion

Religion is superior to ethics and philosophy. It is higher than culture and the knowledge of good and evil. It surpasses these others because it brings in God. Religion looks to God for help. Religion promotes the worship of God and asks His help in doing good and forsaking evil. Yet it has not forsaken philosophy nor rejected culture. It has rather adopted the positive aspects of culture and incorporated ethical teachings into its structure.

These five things — the knowledge of good and evil, culture, philosophy, ethics, and religion — are the controlling factors of fallen mankind. Wherever we may have been born and raised, we have been educated along the lines of these five things. Whether we are from the West or from the East, whether we are from one race or another, we have been taught from childhood the knowledge of good and evil. Our cultural backgrounds may seem quite different from others', but the differences are only superficial. We have all been taught, for example, to honor our parents, to be honest, and to love others. This is our common cultural heritage, though we may have learned it in Europe, in Asia, or in Africa. The same is true of philosophy and ethics. Though they may have arisen in widely separated parts of the world, in essence all the philosophies and ethical teachings are concerned with promoting the good and rejecting the evil. They are the same in principle.

As for religion, there are only three major ones: Judaism, Islam, and Catholicism. Islam, the Moslem religion, is closely related to Judaism. In fact, the Koran, the Moslem bible, has many parts very similar to the Old Testament and to some of the New Testament. In Christianity Catholicism has developed as a religion. Judaism, Islam, and Catholicism all had their origins in the Bible. They worship the same God.

In India there is Buddhism, but we do not call that a religion because the Buddha is not a god. The Chinese follow mainly the ethical teachings of Confucius, which is not a religion either.

All religion utilizes God. It looks to God to help promote and uplift culture, to improve people's knowledge of good and evil, to strengthen their philosophy, and to enable them to live by their ethical teachings.

This is the situation in which we were born and raised. We have been taught to live by the knowledge of good and evil. We act according to our culture. We are influenced by philosophy. We try to follow ethical teachings. We are governed and directed by our religious upbringing.

Before you were saved, your behavior was probably loose and sinful. Once you were saved, you repented and regretted your past. You tried not to do anything wrong. You asked God to help you not to sin nor to offend others, but to strengthen you to live in a morally upright way. You wanted always to walk in His presence.

The result of our background and then of our Christian experience is that we have become people living a certain way. The way we live is to do good, to try to walk in the presence of God, and to glorify Him. Dear saints, this is the wrong way to live! It is Satan's subtle deceit. It is not God's intention for us to live an upright life. He does not want us to be religious. His intention for us is neither to be good nor to be evil. Both good and bad are out of His intention.

What, then, is God's intention? It is that He come into us and become our life. He becomes one with us and makes us one with Him that we may live Him. We are to live God, not good! He is not after good men but God-men! God wants to be our life and nature. He wants us to be His expression. He is not satisfied to have us merely express what is good; nor does He want us to express what is evil. We are to express simply God Himself: this is His intention.

This very God, in order to accomplish His intention, became a man. He went through incarnation, human living, and crucifixion. Then He became in resurrection the life-giving Spirit. Through incarnation He entered into man; through resurrection He brought man into Him.

Now He is in us, and we are in Him. We must no longer live according to the knowledge of good and evil. We are not to follow the dictates of culture. Philosophy is under our feet. Ethical teachings we must disregard. Religion is not for us. We no longer have any need of these things. In their place we have the very Spirit who is the ultimate consummation of the Triune God!

When we turn from these other things in which we were raised and educated, we are left with only this all-inclusive Spirit. Religion, ethics, philosophy, culture, the knowledge of good and evil — all are gone. Only the living God is left. We know Him as the Spirit. He is the Spirit, indwelling our spirit. Rather than practicing the presence of God, we practice being one spirit with the Lord. When we live, He lives. When He lives, we live. We and He are one.

TRANSFORMATION

We must remember, however, that we are tripartite. It is indeed wonderful to have the Spirit with our spirit, but we have also a soul and a body. The spirit is the center of our being, while the body is the circumference. In between is the soul. The soul occupies a great part of our being. The Triune God is in our spirit, but our soul may contain very little Christ. Our soul may be occupied by self alone. While we are saying, "Praise the Lord for the Spirit in my spirit!" our mind, the biggest part of the soul, is still full of self. Our emotion, another part of the soul, is fully in our hands. Our will, the third part of the soul, remains untouched.

Our spirit has been regenerated, but our soul is still old and unchanged. We need transformation. Romans 12:2 says, "And do not be conformed to this age, but be transformed by the renewing of the mind, that you may prove by testing what the will of God is, that which is good and well-pleasing and perfect."

To be conformed to this age is to be modern. Wanting to be modern comes from the soul. Suppose you look at the advertisements in the newspapers. Your interest is aroused by the fashions they show. Your emotion finds some styles appealing. Your mind begins to figure out how much money you can afford to spend. Your will makes a decision to go and buy a certain one.

If this is your practice, you are conformed to this age. Do not be conformed to this age! To be conformed to this age is to get the things that satisfy the soul. The soul likes fashions and color variations. It is never satisfied.

". . . But be transformed by the renewing of the mind." The renewing of the mind indicates that transformation is in the soul, because the mind is the leading part of the soul. For our soul to be transformed, what is first needed is the renewal of the mind. These are two different words: conformed and transformed. To be conformed does not require that anything new be added to our inner being; it is an outward matter. To be transformed, in contrast, requires that a new element be added inwardly to us.

Conformity is mostly a matter of appearance. About fifteen years ago many young people were attracted to the hippie movement in California. It did not take any great effort for them to become hippies. All they had to do was to let their hair grow long and stop taking showers! They did not need a special element added to them. Simply by adopting that kind of life style, they were conformed.

Transformation is not outward like conformity. Suppose someone's face is quite pale. He needs to be transformed. The answer to his problem is not makeup. What he needs is to eat nourishing food in a regular way. As this food is digested and assimilated into his blood, its elements will become part of his cells. These new elements will gradually transform his paleness into a healthful color. By eating properly, his being has been changed. The old has been discharged and the new added to replace the old. No color has been outwardly added to his skin; the change in color has been inwardly brought about. Transformation is like this.

What is the new element that brings about this inward change? It is Christ, the Triune God, the all-inclusive Spirit. At first this element is only in our spirit. He is confined there, with no way to enter our mind, emotion, and will. If we do not allow Him to spread, our spirit becomes a prison to Him. We need the teaching about transformation by the renewing of the mind. The Spirit wants to spread into our soul, thus adding the new divine element to replace the self. When this new element replacing the old is added to our soul, there will be a change in our mind, emotion, and will.

Of all the books in the Bible, only the writings of Paul speak of transformation. Part of the completing ministry is that we need to be transformed. This change in our inner being comes about by the divine element being added to us to replace the self.

THE WAY TO BE TRANSFORMED

"Now the Lord is the Spirit: and where the Spirit of the Lord is, there is liberty. But we all, with unveiled face beholding and reflecting as a mirror the glory of the Lord, are being transformed into the same image from glory to glory, even as from the Lord Spirit" (2 Cor. 3:17-18, lit.).

What is the liberty referred to here? It is freedom from the knowledge of good and evil, from culture, from philosophy, from ethical teachings, and from religion. Where the Spirit of the Lord is, we shall be bound no longer by these things. In Paul's time many believers were still under the bondage of law. They needed to be free from the law and from the Jewish religion. In our day the Chinese believers need to be liberated from the teachings of Confucius. All of us need to be set free from religion. We all need to be cleared out. Nothing should be left in us of the old knowledge of good and evil, the old culture, the old philosophy, the old ethical teachings, and the old religion.

Verse 18 says we are like mirrors with unveiled faces. All these veils have been taken away. All five layers need to be removed. Even if only one veil remains, our vision is impaired. The things in the Bible we cannot see, even though they are there. This is why many Christians do not see beyond the words when they read the Bible. Their eyes are veiled by all these layers.

Every layer needs to be removed. Then we as mirrors with unveiled face beholding and reflecting the Lord, are being transformed. The way to be transformed is to remove the veil of the knowledge of good and evil, of culture, of philosophy, of ethical teaching, and of religion. Then we can look at the Lord with unveiled face and have Him shine into our being.

If you want to take a picture, you must be sure to take the cover off the camera lens. Then, when you touch the shutter, the light shines in and the picture is taken. The same is true of you. If your face is unveiled and you look to the Lord, He Himself will be shined into your mind, emotion, and will, as well as your spirit. Something divine has shined into us, replacing the old and thus causing a change. This change is called transformation in Paul's completing ministry. It is the Spirit spreading out from our spirit into our soul to occupy and saturate every part of it.

THE PURPOSE OF TRANSFORMATION

Transformation is for the building of God. Without it there is no possibility of His gaining a building. Even though our spirit has been regenerated, there is no way for believers to be built into one as long as our soul is full of self. What is the self? Opinion is the self in expression. As long as we are full of our differing opinions, we cannot be one.

If, however, we allow the Spirit to spread out, one by one our opinions will go. As we are all transformed, we become one. Gradually through transformation all of us are delivered from our opinions, and we become one, not only in our spirit but also in our soul. This oneness is the building, which is the purpose of transformation.

A message given by Witness Lee
in Stuttgart, Germany, April 12, 1980

Published by
Living Stream Ministry
1853 W. Ball Road, Anaheim, CA 92804, U.S.A.
(714) 991-4681

THE COMPLETING MINISTRY OF PAUL

GROWTH IN LIFE
THROUGH THE TRANSFORMATION OF OUR SOUL
FOR THE BUILDING UP OF THE BODY

Scripture Reading: 2 Cor. 3:18; Rom. 12:2; Phil. 2:2;
1 Cor. 3:6-12; Eph. 4:12-16

The verses above deal mainly with the matter of life and its issue, which is the building. This is actually the theme of the whole New Testament. Life is simply the Triune God, who, after passing through a lengthy process, became the Spirit of life. As such, He is life to us. The building is the church, the Body of Christ. This building comes out of life. The church is the issue of the divine life; its ultimate consummation is the New Jerusalem.

Once we receive this life, the New Testament tells us, it begins to grow within us, to saturate us, to transform us, and to build us together as God's dwelling place. In this age His dwelling place is the church; in the eternal age it is the New Jerusalem. The dwelling place is the issue of God's being life to us. As His life within us grows, we are transformed; the purpose of this transformation is the building up of God's dwelling place. Growth, transformation, and building are the crucial points in the New Testament. Nonetheless, they have been largely overlooked by most Christians, who instead pay attention to lesser things.

TRANSFORMATION

Transformation follows regeneration. Our spiritual life began with regeneration. When we believed on the Lord Jesus and called on His name, He as the life-giving Spirit entered into our spirit and regenerated it. Since then, the Triune God has indwelt our spirit. Thus, in spirit we are one with Him.

Now there is the need for Him to spread from our spirit into our soul. When He as the life-giving Spirit has spread into our soul and saturated it, we are transformed. Transformation is the saturation of our soul by the Triune God. Regeneration is a birth in our spirit; transformation, a saturation in our soul.

Transformation is a metabolic change. In the physical body metabolism refers to the processes in cells by which old materials are discharged and new are added. This change, applied to the soul, is called in the New Testament transformation (2 Cor. 3:18; Rom. 12:2). To apply makeup may result in a change in appearance, but it is merely an outward, not a metabolic, change. To have a better skin color because of an improved diet, on the other hand, is the result of a metabolic process. New elements are organically assimilated by the body, replacing the old. Transformation is a change in life, not merely in appearance. The divine element is added to us; this discharges the old human element. This organic change takes place in our soul.

Our spirit, then, needs regeneration; our soul, transformation. In all the churches the saints should be concerned about this metabolic change in life through the spreading of the divine Spirit.

DISTINGUISHING BETWEEN SOUL AND SPIRIT

Before we go on, I would like to be sure we are all clear as to the difference between the soul and the spirit. In the center of our being is our spirit. Around the spirit is the soul. Then the outermost part is the body. We can illustrate it like this:

It is the clear teaching of Scripture that man is tri-partite (1 Thes. 5:23). Nonetheless, there are two schools of theology which have arisen on this subject. One believes, as the Bible teaches, that man is a trichotomy; that is, he is made up of spirit, soul, and body. The other school maintains that man is a dichotomy; that is, he has an outer part, the body, and an inner part, the spirit or soul. In this latter school spirit, soul, and heart are considered synonyms.

Such an unscriptural view of man is revealed in the New American Standard Version of the Bible. In Philippians 2:2, where the literal rendering is "joined in soul," this version has "united in *spirit*." Again, in Philippians 2:20, where Paul says that Timothy is "like-souled" (lit.), this version has "of kindred *spirit*." To translate soul as spirit is inexcusable. It clearly indicates that the translators saw no difference between soul and spirit.

A number of Bible teachers do not differentiate between soul and spirit. I once met a missionary from the Brethren who strongly argued with me that there was no difference between soul and spirit. I called his attention to 1 Thessalonians 5:23, where Paul mentions "your whole spirit and soul and body." Surely Paul would not have put "and" between them if they were the same. To my astonishment, he replied that no matter what the Bible said, spirit and soul were still one and the same! That was the end of the argument; I told him if he did not believe what the Bible said, there was no point in further talk.

To be born of the Spirit in our spirit is the beginning. Our spirit has been regenerated, but the soul is still empty. The divine, indwelling Spirit expects to spread into our soul, that is, into our mind, emotion, and will. He wants to saturate our inward parts.

GROWTH IN LIFE

For many years I tried to find out what is meant by the growth in life. The Bible does emphasize the need for us to grow in life, or for the divine life to grow in us. I could not come to a clear understanding of what this meant or how it could come about, even after studying the Bible, reading various spiritual books, and considering my own experiences.

Now I realize that the real growth in life is the transformation of the soul.

In the parable of the ten virgins (Matt. 25:1-13), the Lord Jesus speaks of their lamps and their vessels. Both the prudent and the foolish had oil in their lamps (see v. 8), but only the prudent took oil in their vessels. Two portions of oil were needed, one for the lamp and the other for the vessel. Proverbs 20:27 says, "The spirit of man is the lamp of the Lord" (lit). The virgins' lamps, then, refer to the spirit. Romans 9:21 and 23 tell us that our being is God's vessel. This means that our soul is the vessel. Those who are saved all have oil in the lamp; that is, we have the Spirit in our spirit. Whether we have an extra portion of oil in our vessel, however, is another question. While the prudent virgins took oil in their vessels, the foolish did not.

Whether we are foolish or prudent, then, depends not on our spirit but upon our soul. Our spirit has been regenerated, but is our soul now saturated with the Spirit? Do we have the extra portion of oil in our vessel? This is a matter we must seriously consider. Now that we have been regenerated, we need to be transformed; that is, we need to grow in life. To grow is to increase. The life abiding in our spirit needs to spread out into our soul until it is saturated. Otherwise, our soul remains natural and old. As the new elements of the divine Spirit enter into our soul, it is organically transformed. This transformation is the growth in life.

There are many Christians who have virtually no growth in life. This is because the indwelling Spirit has been given no opportunity to spread into their soul and saturate it.

A FARM AND A BUILDING

Where does the Scripture indicate that transformation and the growth in life are one and the same? First Corinthians 3 says: "I planted, Apollos watered, but God made to grow. . . . You are God's farm, God's building. . . . But if anyone builds on the foundation gold, silver, precious stones, wood, grass, stubble, the work of each shall become manifest" (vv. 6, 9, 12-13).

Paul says that we are God's farm, God's building. We are here to grow Christ. Paul planted, Apollos watered, and God gave the growth. These terms all pertain to the matter of growth. How is growth the same as transformation? We are also a building, with gold, silver, precious stones. We start out as plants growing on God's farm, but the end result is gold, silver, and precious stones. Is this not transformation? Frail plants are transformed into such solid things! It is possible, we are warned, for the result to be wood, grass, and stubble, suitable only for burning. Yet we may be transformed into another category, that of gold, silver, and precious stones.

Suppose we take three brothers. They are young, perhaps having only recently come into the church life. We may consider them as plants. One is a small tree, another is a shrub, and the third a tender flower. They are growing on God's farm, the church. See how delicate they are! They cannot take any kind of harsh treatment or damage. Yet, though they are young, they are growing. The Lord expects that one day this small tree will change into gold, this shrub will become silver, and this flower will be a precious stone.

This flower, this shrub, and this small tree look lovely to us today. Suppose, however, that after three years we find them still the same. They have not grown and been transformed. They may be lovely to look at, but they are not suitable for building material. Can a house be built with flowers? Can a little tree be used for a doorpost? Can a shrub be part of a wall? There could not be such a building! Nor can these be the building materials of the New Jerusalem. The New Jerusalem is built of gold with walls of precious stone and gates of pearl. God's building is not with fragile flowers, delicate shrubs, and tender saplings!

These three brothers all need to change. They need an organic, metabolic transformation. After three years we do not want to find this brother still a flower, lovely to look at but useless for building. We want him to be a precious stone, even though the beautiful blossoms are gone. We want to see this shrub changed into a pearl perhaps, solid and transparent. This tree also needs to be transformed, perhaps into gold as pure as glass.

Dear saints, are you content to be trees, shrubs, and flowers? Or do you long to be precious stones? On this "farm" in Stuttgart, which do you have? I believe you have a variety growing here. There are plants, but also some gold, silver, and precious stones.

This farm that is also a building illustrates the way the indwelling Spirit spreads from our spirit to permeate our soul and thus transforms us.

ONENESS

When we meet together for the church life, we can praise the Lord that He has regenerated us and that His Spirit indwells our spirit. Problems arise, however, with our soul, which is full of our opinions and natural concepts. Suppose five saints come together from different countries. Can they be built together? When they pray, sing, call on the Lord, and say hallelujah, they enjoy being one in spirit. Once the prayer is over, however, and they begin to talk together, the spirit is forgotten. Out comes French opinion. English opinion. German opinion. Chinese opinion. Japanese opinion. When their eyes are shut in prayer, they are one. When they open their eyes and look at each other, they journey from their spirit to their soul. There is this difference of opinion not only among different nationalities. Within a country, say, the United States, can the Texas brothers be one with those in California? Can those in California be one with those in New York? Even couples cannot be one. There is the man's point of view, which differs from the way a woman looks at things.

How can all these differences be resolved? There is no natural way to work them out. We must let the indwelling Spirit spread and saturate our soul. Then spontaneously we shall be one. We shall be joined in soul (Phil. 2:2). The natural concepts will give place to the spreading Spirit. This is the way we grow in life. Out of this growth in life comes oneness. We can be built together with all the saints.

Without the spreading of the Spirit into your soul, your oneness with others is of short duration. If you visit Hong Kong, for example, you will be warmly received and at first feel happy to be there. Within a very short time, however, you will realize how differently they do things from the way you think they should be done. Before many days go by, you will be offended. While you are here at home, you shout, "Hallelujah for the one new man!" but when you are in a new environment, the new man is cut into pieces by the concepts you still hold.

Your soul is still not transformed. You are still living in your soul, which remains old and natural. This is the hindrance to the new man. Will you allow the indwelling Spirit to thoroughly saturate your soul so that it is organically transformed? Will you give the Spirit the freedom to permeate your soul as well as your spirit? If He does, whether you go to Ghana, or the Philippines, or Brazil, you will have no problem. The base of your opinion will have been destroyed. With your soul saturated by the indwelling Spirit, you are one with the new man. You are built up in the Body. Whatever locality you visit, whomever you meet, there is no problem on your side.

When this is true of the saints all over the world, there will be the new man. The Body will be built up.

THE GOAL AND THE WAY TO REACH IT

Ephesians 4:12-16 tells us that the building up of the Body of Christ depends on the growth in life. "For the perfecting of the saints unto the work of ministry, unto the building up of the Body of Christ; until we all arrive at the oneness of the faith and of the full knowledge of the Son of God, at a full-grown man, at the measure of the stature of the fullness of Christ, that we may be no longer babes . . . but . . . may grow up into Him in all things, Who is the Head, Christ, out from Whom all the Body, fitted and knit together through every joint of the supply, according to the operation in measure of each one part, causes the growth of the Body unto the building up of itself in love."

This "growing up into Him in all things" comes about through our soul's being saturated with the Spirit. There must be "the growth of the Body" for the Lord to have the new man. This is the goal the Lord is pursuing. When His Body is built up, He will have the new man on earth to carry out God's eternal purpose. Let us pray for this to be realized and offer ourselves to Him for this. "Lord, spread Yourself from my spirit into my soul. Saturate my soul. Transform me metabolically. I want to be organically changed." After some time we shall be transformed by the growth in life. Then we shall be built into the Body and be members of the new man. As this happens in many of us throughout the whole earth, the new man will come into being. This is the Lord's goal. Let us be one with Him in pursuing this.

A message given by Witness Lee
in Stuttgart, Germany, April 13, 1980

Published by
Living Stream Ministry
1853 W. Ball Road, Anaheim, CA 92804, U.S.A.
(714) 991-4681

THE COMPLETING MINISTRY OF PAUL

MESSAGE TEN

THE CENTRAL VISION

(1)

GOD AS OUR CONTENTS

Scripture Reading: Col. 1:25-27; Rom. 9:23-24; 2 Cor. 4:7; Eph. 3:19b; 4:6; Phil. 2:14; Heb. 13:20-21; 1 Tim. 3:16

COMPLETING THE WORD OF GOD

Very few Christians have seen Paul's completing ministry. This term, the completing ministry, is based upon Colossians 1:25, where Paul says he was commissioned "to complete the word of God." To complete the word of God means to complete the revelation of God. No doubt the King James Version's rendering of "complete the word of God" as "fulfil the word of God" has somewhat obscured the real meaning.

Without Paul's writings the revelation of God is not complete. If his fourteen Epistles, from Romans through Hebrews, were taken from the Bible, it would no doubt still be a marvelous book. Think how wonderful Genesis is! How great a book Exodus is! Yet without Paul's Epistles we could not have had the wonderful Life-studies on Genesis and Exodus. Why? Though Genesis and Exodus are admirable, without Paul's writings they lack completion.

THE MYSTERY OF GOD

Notice the two verses which follow Colossians 1:25 about the completing of the word of God: "The mystery which has been hidden from the ages and from the generations, but now has been manifested to His saints; to whom God willed to make known what are the riches of the glory of this mystery among the nations, which is Christ in you, the hope of glory" (vv. 26-27). Grammatically speaking, "the mystery" is in apposition with "to complete the word of God." The completion of the word of God is the mystery. This mystery, which was hidden but is now manifested, concerns "Christ in you, the hope of glory."

Well, you may wonder, does not Matthew tell us about Christ? And is Christ not the subject of the other Gospels? Surely every book of the New Testament is about Christ. None of these books except Paul's, however, say that Christ is God's mystery. Matthew deals with the mystery of the kingdom of God, but does not present Christ as God's mystery. Mark and Luke make no mention of this matter. Even in John's Gospel the word mystery is not to be found. It does occur in his Revelation, but it is not as clearly mentioned as in Paul's Epistles. Only Paul uses the word mystery for Christ and for His Body.

THE SOURCE AND ISSUE OF THIS MYSTERY

Christ is a mystery. What is the source of Christ as a mystery? It is surely God. Both the Jews and the Moslems claim to know God. They are of a similar origin, in that their faith is based on the Old Testament. (The Moslem Bible, the Koran, is largely an imitation of the Old Testament, with some changes.) The God in whom the Jews and Moslems believe is the God of the Old Testament. In the New Testament our God is the God in Christ and through Christ. To be a Christian is to come into Christ and through Him into God. God is embodied in this Christ. The fullness of the Godhead dwells in Him bodily (Col. 2:9). God's entire being is embodied in Christ. My body is the embodiment of me; if you want to find where I am, you will find me in this body. Similarly, our Christ is the embodiment of God. If anyone has a God who is apart from Christ, he must be like a Jew or a Moslem. God, then, is the source of this mystery.

What is the issue of this mystery? This mystery comes out of God and issues in the church, including all the believers of Christ. In the whole universe this is the mystery! Without such a word the Bible is not complete. This completion of the word is this great mystery: Christ as the mystery of God and the church as the mystery of Christ. These two comprise the mystery of the ages. They are unfolded to us in Paul's completing ministry.

GOD NOT ONLY THE CREATOR

In this message and in the next two we want to consider what the focus is of Paul's completing ministry. We have elsewhere referred to Ephesians, Galatians, Philippians, and Colossians as the heart of the divine revelation. In these messages we shall discuss the central vision, the focal point, of Paul's completing ministry.

We have three messages on this subject because Paul's ministry has three main points: God, Christ, and the church. This message will be concerning God. However, I would first like to comment on Christ, the subject of our second message. The matter of the Trinity is the most puzzling in the whole Bible. If we want to know Christ, we must understand this puzzle. If we do not understand how God is in Christ, we know neither God nor Christ. If we do not know how Christ is related to, even identical with, the Spirit, we do not know either Christ or the Spirit.

GOD WANTING A CONTAINER

When Paul refers to God, he of course says that God is the Creator (Rom. 1:25), but this is not his central point. The Old Testament has already told us this. Let us consider Romans 9:23-24: "And what if He should make known the riches of His glory upon vessels of mercy, which He had before prepared unto glory, even us, whom He has also called, not only from among the Jews, but also from among the nations?" We are here called vessels. God has chosen us to be His vessels, vessels of mercy unto glory.

This implies and indicates that God wants to be contained; He wants a container for Himself.

Man is a vessel. Firstly, our body is a vessel. Every day we fill it with food, water, and air. Day by day we eat, drink, and breathe. We eat probably three times a day, besides snacks. We drink more times a day. In addition, we are continuously breathing. Whatever else we are doing, we keep breathing. Without it, we graduate from living! By eating, drinking, and breathing we fill ourselves. Our outer man, then, is a vessel.

MAN A VESSEL TO CONTAIN GOD

Our inner man is also a vessel. God has created us as vessels to contain Him. "We have this treasure in earthen vessels, that the excellency of the power may be of God, and not of us," Paul tells us in 2 Corinthians 4:7. From verses 5 and 6 we know that the treasure is God Himself in Christ, who has sown Himself into us, the earthen vessels. These verses are familiar to us, yet we do not live as those who have God as their contents.

Seldom does the thought cross our mind that we are a vessel to contain God. All too often, however, we entertain the thought that we must behave rightly, courteously, humbly, and inoffensively. Day after day we are sorry not to be more obedient to our parents, more pleasant to our classmates, and kinder to our sister or brother. We may think along even more spiritual lines, about getting up early for morning watch or spending more time to read the Bible. Such thoughts are commonplace to us. But how about the thought that we are vessels to contain God? Does this thought occur to us? We may obey our parents and love our sister but not have God contained in us. If so, we are like an empty box, trying to please others but apart from God. It is not only the unbelievers who are on the wrong track. It is not only other Christians who are off. We who are in the Lord's recovery are also often off the track. Whenever we think in terms of loving others or being kind, without realizing that we were ordained to contain God, we too are missing the mark. We must learn to turn away from all such considerations of behavior and care only to be filled with God.

God is illustrated in the Bible as food, water, and air. We must take Him in and be filled with Him just as we take in the food we eat, the water we drink, and the air we breathe. Over these past twenty years a number of hymns have been composed among us which speak of eating and drinking Christ and of breathing God in. The thought in these hymns is missing from other Christian hymnals. To some people the thought of eating God is rough and unacceptable. We cannot blame them for thinking this way; they are short of revelation.

We have been not only created by God, then, but also chosen by Him to be vessels of His mercy. And not only are we vessels of mercy; we are also vessels prepared unto glory. It is only Paul's writings, of all the twenty-seven books of the New Testament, which convey the thought that we are vessels to contain God. In the next message we shall cover how this God could be contained in us. From Romans 8 we shall see how God must be the Spirit and that this Spirit must be the Spirit of Christ. Then God can be in us as our contents.

FILLED UNTO ALL THE FULLNESS OF GOD

Ephesians 4:6 says, "One God and Father of all, Who is over all and through all and in all." The Father is not only over us; He is not only through us; He is also in us. This preposition in does not mean merely with; it means that God is within us. God is housing Himself in us, as Paul writes elsewhere. The Chinese translation of this verse says that He dwells in us.

Ephesians 3:19b says, "That you may be filled unto all the fullness of God." To be filled unto all God's fullness means to be filled unto all that God is. This fullness dwells in Christ (Col. 1:19; 2:9). Through His indwelling, Christ imparts the fullness of God into our being. This makes us God's expression. The fullness of God implies that the riches of what He is become His expression. When the riches are in Him, they are His riches; when they are expressed, they become His fullness. All that God is should be our contents. We should be so filled with Him that we become His fullness, His expression.

To become God's fullness is in a category entirely apart from being kind and humble. These past three years I have several times repented for being outwardly blameless while I was not filled with the Lord. "Lord," I have prayed, "forgive me. I failed You today. I enjoyed being with that brother, but I was not filled with You. I loved certain ones, but I was not filled with You. I helped the church, but I was not filled with You. I talked to the elders and they were helped, but I was not filled with You. Forgive me for all the good things I did apart form You as my contents." We all need to become aware of this distinction between being good and being filled with the Lord.

GOD OPERATING IN US

"For it is God Who operates in you both the willing and the working for His good pleasure" (Phil. 2:13). What does this verse tell us God is doing? Does it say that it is God who inspires us from the heavens to will and to do? Is the almighty God reaching down from His throne to stir us up? No! God is operating in us. The Greek word for operate has no precise English equivalent, though the word energize comes from it and somewhat conveys the meaning. The thought in this verse is that God is moving, acting, working, rubbing within us. Our God is continuously working in us. We must think of Him not as far off on the throne but as within, constantly touching, moving, rubbing, and bothering us.

The very next verse says, "Do all things without murmurings and reasonings" (Phil. 2:14). While you are murmuring, God is operating in you. While you are reasoning, He is moving in you. He tells you to stop, but you reply, "In a minute!" Though you will not stop, even when the minute is up, God continues His operating in you. His working within never ceases. This is our God. You may say such a God is too small. The Jews may believe that their God is great and exalted on the throne, but I like having such a small God. He is far more practical and relevant to my everyday situation. One bird in hand is worth a thousand birds in the air! My God is within me, bothering all the time!

GOD EQUIPPING US

"Now the God of peace Who brought up from among the dead our Lord Jesus, the great Shepherd of the sheep, by the blood of an eternal covenant, equip you in every good work for the doing of His will, doing in us that which is well-pleasing in His sight through Jesus Christ, to Whom be the glory forever and ever, Amen" (Heb. 13:20-21). If we were writing such a prayer, we would probably say something like, "May the God of peace equip you to do good works that you may glorify Him"! Why did Paul insert such a long modifier, "Who brought up from among the dead our Lord Jesus, the great Shepherd of the sheep, by the blood of an eternal covenant"?

The old covenant was enacted by the blood of the sacrifices. The blood opened the door for the new covenant also to come in. The new covenant is to write God's nature into our being as the law of life, to give us a new spirit, and even to put us into God the Spirit. Whose blood is the blood of an eternal covenant? It is the blood of Christ. This blood ushers in His resurrection. In Christ's resurrection God comes into us.

How does God equip us? It is not by being in the heavens outside us. He equips us by coming into us. He can come into us through the resurrection of Christ. The resurrection is here through the shedding of His blood. This God, who is brought to us through the resurrection, is now equipping us "through Jesus Christ." God is not reaching down from the heavens to stir us up. He is "doing in us what is well-pleasing in His sight through Jesus Christ." Our God through Christ in His resurrection has come into us. Now He is "doing" in us still in resurrection through Christ.

GOD MANIFESTED IN THE FLESH

"Great is the mystery of godliness, Who was manifested in the flesh, vindicated in the Spirit, seen by angels, preached among the nations, believed on in the world, taken up in glory" (1 Tim. 3:16).

This God has been manifested in the flesh. Such a statement refers not only to Christ but also to the church. The church is a group of men of flesh who manifest God. It is God manifested in corporate flesh. How could God be thus manifested? It is by our taking Him in and being filled with Him.

This is your God and my God. It was Paul's God. Before his conversion, Paul's God was far away in the heavens. Now the very God of the apostle is the God that in resurrection through Jesus Christ is making His home in your being, that He might saturate you, even express Himself from within you.

OUR OPPOSING NATURAL CONCEPTS

This is the central vision concerning God which Paul presents to us. We have our own natural concepts, however, which are other than this. There are eleven of these which I would like to point out.

"Worshipping" God

Man's natural concept concerning God is that He is to be worshipped. Man as the creature must pay homage to his almighty Creator. This is a noble idea, but it is somewhat off. God's heart is not satisfied by those who worship Him in an outward way. His heart's longing is to have man for His container.

When the Lord Jesus spoke to the sinful Samaritan woman in John 4, she turned the topic of conversation from her sinful living to the worship of God. In the Lord's conversation with her He indicated that to worship God she must drink of the living water which is God in Christ through the Spirit. The proper worship of God is to drink Him. The more we drink of Him, the more we are worshipping Him. To worship God without taking Him in as our life supply is poor. God cannot be satisfied with that. The external worship of God is simply man's natural concept.

Being Ethical

Man was not created a beast or a monkey. He has a much higher form of life. Thus he has the concept that he should behave according to a high standard of morality. This desire to be ethical is natural and also somewhat off. It is not that God wants you to behave immorally; His standard is far higher than yours. Nonetheless, the concept of being ethical is contrary to God's desire for man.

Being Religious

Man wants to do things for God. He wants to carry out his religious obligations. Yet what he does for God he does apart from God. All man's doing for God yet without Him is off.

Being Devotional

You may have noticed that in the Lord's recovery we do not speak of having a devotional time. To be devotional without the Spirit is also off.

Being Pious

To be pious is to love and fear God and to try to behave in a way that is according to what God is. The concept of being pious is very strong among earnest Christians. In Germany there was a group who were called Pietists, who sought to practice piety in all aspects of their living.

James 1:27 speaks of "pure religion and undefiled before God and the Father." Some would quote this verse in protest to what I am saying. How deeply ingrained is this concept that we must act in a pious, religious manner! However, to be pious without the Spirit is also off from the central line of God's economy.

Being Holy

Denominations have been formed around this concept. Those who belong to them are called holiness people. What do they mean by being holy? Their members are not supposed to wear short skirts. They must not use makeup. They must be sure their bodies are well covered. Such is their concept of being holy.

Being Scriptural

The Brethren have this as their standard. They evaluate things as being scriptural or unscriptural. This is right. However, you may be true to your understanding of the Scriptures, yet, if you are void of the reality of the Spirit, you are nonetheless off from the central vision of the Apostle Paul's completing ministry.

Being Spiritual

Among Christians there is the concept that we must be spiritual. What is actually meant by this word is hard to say.

Having Power

Some Christians are impressed by those whom they regard as having pentecostal power. A certain evangelist, in their eyes, is a powerful speaker. He may be powerful, but he is still off in life from the central vision of Paul's completing ministry.

Valuing the Miraculous

Healing, speaking in tongues, filling teeth, and leg-lengthening are all found in today's Christianity. Those who are into the miraculous are off.

Serving God

There is the widely held concept of working for God, of going to the mission field to win souls for Christ. This concept also has a great discrepancy compared with Paul's completing ministry.

THE OLD TESTAMENT CONCEPT

There was recently a message given by a visiting brother which I am sure you found very helpful. He said that the garden of Eden was a garden of joy, not only because of the tree of life and the flowing river, but even more because God was there walking with man. Later I spoke with this brother and pointed out to him that his emphasis should have been just the opposite. The garden of Eden was a paradise not only because God was there walking with man, but far more because the tree of life was there, indicating that God one day would enter into man to be his life. To walk with God is far inferior to having Him live in us as our life and our food. Yes, God did walk with Adam in the garden, but God had more than that in mind. His ultimate purpose was to enter into Adam, to be Adam's life and life supply.

In "The Practice of the Presence of God" Brother Lawrence teaches that we need to practice living in God's presence all day long. Such a teaching is according to the Old Testament. In the New Testament there is no such term as living in God's presence. The New Testament tells us to walk in spirit (Rom. 8:4). Rather than practicing the presence of God, we live one spirit with Him (1 Cor. 6:17). Do you see the difference? Walking with God seems wonderful, but it is an Old Testament concept. In the New Testament we are one with God. When I walk, He walks with me; when He walks, I walk with Him.

Too many Christians today treasure the still small voice; they think this is the way the Lord leads them. Again, this is an Old Testament concept (1 Kings 19:12). There is no need for us to listen for a still small voice. We have the indwelling (Rom. 8:11) and the anointing, which abides in us (1 John 2:27). This is far higher than the still small voice. In the time of the Old Testament God had not yet entered into man. In our day, however, God in resurrection through Christ has entered into us as the Spirit, is now indwelling us, is one with us, and has made us one spirit with Himself!

When you hear a message inspiring you to seek to have a walk with God, you feel that you have been greatly helped. Yes, you have been helped, but you have been helped to be frustrated from getting onto the central vision of the Apostle Paul's completing ministry. The thought of walking with God is altogether other than the central vision of the Apostle Paul's completing ministry. If Paul had been listening to that message, he would have interrupted and said, "Brother, don't go on. We are not living today in the garden of Eden. We are in the church!"

I realize it is hard for you to catch what I am saying. The old concepts have covered your eyes, occupied your thoughts, and dominated your way of living. You came from that background. You remember how Enoch walked with God for three hundred years. You recall how Elijah listened for the still small voice. How you admire them! How you wish you could be like them!

Elijah would say to you, "Foolish one! It is for *me* to envy *you*. Even John the Baptist was greater than I; but you are far greater even than John. Why would you want to be like me? John the Baptist was greater than I because he was closer to Christ. You are not only closer to Christ; you are one spirit with Him! Am I greater than you? I want to follow you. I will gladly give up the still small voice. I want to walk according to the indwelling, according to the abiding, according to the anointing, according to spirit!"

May the Lord open our eyes to see what is off and what is not off. All the "off" concepts fit our natural mentality. It is not easy to see the difference.

A message given by Witness Lee
in Anaheim, California, April 17, 1981

© 1981 Living Stream Ministry

Published by
Living Stream Ministry
1853 W. Ball Road, Anaheim, CA 92804, U.S.A.
(714) 991-4681

THE COMPLETING MINISTRY OF PAUL

MESSAGE ELEVEN

THE CENTRAL VISION

(2)

CHRIST AS THE MYSTERY OF GOD

Scripture Reading: Col. 1:25-27; 2:2, 9; Rom. 9:5; 1 Cor. 15:45b; 2 Cor. 3:17-18; Rom. 8:9-11; Eph. 3:14-19; 2 Cor. 13:14

Before we continue with the central vision of the Apostle Paul's completing ministry, I would like to tell you some of my history in the hope that you will see my gradual realization of the importance of this vision.

A GRADUAL ENLIGHTENING

I was born into organized Christianity. After I grew up, I got saved. It was a marvelous conversion. I began to seek the Lord. I loved the Bible. Then I was attracted to the Brethren assembly. It was their familiarity with the Bible that drew me. I stayed with them for seven and a half years. I learned their teachings on prophecy from Daniel, Matthew, 2 Thessalonians, and Revelation.

We were also taught about the Old Testament types and their fulfillment in the New. Furthermore, we were repeatedly charged not to do anything that was not scriptural. We must not celebrate Christmas nor birthdays; both were unscriptural. Again and again we heard that this was scriptural and that that was not scriptural.

Never did I hear a word concerning God's operating in us. Their Bible seemed not to contain Philippians 2:13: "For it is God Who operates in you." Hebrews 13:21 was also missing: that the God of peace is "doing in us that which is well-pleasing in His sight through Jesus Christ." In the famous Brethren teaching nothing was ever said about God in us. About Christ's indwelling us. About the indwelling Spirit. Occasionally there would be mention of the inspiration of the Holy Spirit.

I recount this background to you so that you can see how the Lord has gradually showed many things to us. I received much help throughout the years from Brother Nee. Then for these past thirty years or so I have been abroad. The vision I see today is far clearer than it was thirty years ago.

LIVING IN THE CIRCLES OF OUR NATURAL CONCEPTS

Nonetheless, however much light we have received, we must all admit that our daily practical life is still around those eleven "off" concepts we covered in the previous message.

Those concepts are like circles, closing us in and limiting us. It is not bad to think about God. Surely there is nothing wrong with worshipping our Creator and trying to please and even glorify Him. Man's ethical concepts also seem commendable. Within man there is a God-created good nature. Of course it was corrupted, but that good element is still in us. On the one hand, we are accustomed to sinning; on the other, we have an intention to do good. These moral inclinations are our ethical concepts. We may, for instance, get angry and quarrel with a member of the family. Later, however, when we are quiet, we are sorry about it and remind ourselves that we must love our family. We may not even quarrel. Under our parents' discipline we have learned not to fight; thus, the annoyance remains inside us. At the breakfast table we may be exasperated with our younger sister. By midmorning, however, the thought comes, "Oh, I must love my sister; she is younger than I." Then we pray, "Lord, help me to love my sister from now on." Later, perhaps while we are at the dining table in the evening, again something comes up, and again the feeling of annoyance comes. Then, perhaps in the meeting that night, we hear something in a message, and the thought returns, "Oh, I must love my sister; Lord, help me to love her." Is not this the story of all of us? It illustrates our ethical behavior.

Then there are our religious, devotional concepts. We want to be pious or holy or spiritual. These are some of the concepts we hold.

We may want to have everything according to the Scriptures. As fundamental Christians, we take the Bible as our guideline. Being scriptural is another concept.

There are also the concepts of wanting to have power and of being able to perform the miraculous. How easy it is to be impressed when we hear of some miraculous happening!

To serve God is another widely held concept. Some thirty or forty years ago many young American Christians devoted themselves to mission work. To be a missionary on the foreign field was considered the highest career.

Do you believe that you are out of these concepts? Day by day all of us, including myself, still travel in all these places. We try to have a good meeting, to stir up the saints to function; this is the concept of having a good meeting. We want to build up the service groups, to get the hall cleaned, the lawn mowed; this is the concept of Saturday morning service. I know the elders might not be happy to hear this; they think I am undoing the church service!

Many times I have confessed, "Lord, I have been good to this one or to that one, but without You." We may be devotional, but apart from the Lord. We may faithfully participate in the church service, but with very little of Him. We are His container; as such, we should take Him as our contents. We should not act in an empty way. As His vessels, we should be filled with Him. Whatever we do must be an expression of Him.

HAVING GOD AS OUR CONTENTS

To do good things for others apart from the Lord is to be in the circles of our natural concepts. There is yet another circle, separate and distinct from these, which we shall call "God in you." It is not a concept; it is having God in us as our contents. This was the subject of our previous message. For this message we shall consider Christ as the mystery of God. Then the final message of this series will be on the church as the mystery of Christ.

As I have been preparing these messages, my heart has been aching. How much do the saints in the recovery have of God as their contents, of Christ as the mystery of God, and of the church as the mystery of Christ? Not very much. In Christianity these points have been much neglected.

If the fourteen Epistles of Paul were removed from the Bible, there would be a great lack. Even if we leave them in, yet remove from them these three points — God as our contents, Christ as God's mystery, and the church as Christ's mystery — Paul's writings would be simply an empty shell.

Nonetheless, dear saints, these are the very points we have missed or neglected. In our daily life, how much attention do we pay to God as our contents? It is not a matter of whether we are defeated or victorious; whether we are common or holy; whether we celebrate birthdays or insist on being scriptural. The question is, Is God our contents? I do not celebrate my grandchildren's birthdays; that saves us work, money, and effort, besides being in accordance with the Scriptures. But these are not the issue; the question is, Where is God? Is He our contents? Sometimes the thought has come to me to buy a present for one of my grandchildren. I would like to reward him for being such a good student and getting top honors. I have not done this, however; not because I wanted to be scriptural, but because God was not there. God is in me, but when I was considering buying my grandson a present, He became absent. I had a sense of His moving in me, but in a way of absenting Himself. There was no still small voice telling me not to do that; only God's moving indicated that He was unhappy. Whatever we do, God must be our contents.

NOT IN THE OLD TESTAMENT

In the whole Old Testament there is no mention that God would be in His chosen people as their contents. The highest charge was that given to Abraham, when God said, "I am the Almighty God; walk before me, and be thou perfect" (Gen. 17:1). The highest possibility was for Abraham to walk before God, to be in God's presence. Abraham even had God pay him a visit in Genesis 18. God stayed with him for part of a day and even ate what Abraham prepared for Him. Have you realized, however, that God did not dwell in Abraham? He did not even dwell in Abraham's tent. The best Abraham could enjoy was a temporary visit. Then God departed. Enoch "walked with God" (Gen. 5:24), but God did not make His home in him.

When we come to the New Testament, however, there is no such term as walking with God. It says instead, "Walk . . . according to spirit" (Rom. 8:4). The spirit in Romans 8 is a mingled person, God mingled with us. God as the Spirit is mingled with our spirit. It is according to this spirit that we must walk. Romans 8 tells us clearly that to walk according to spirit means to walk in God, in the Triune God. How is this possible? It is because the Triune God is in us.)

John 14:23 says, "If anyone loves Me, he will keep My word, and My Father will love him, and We will come to him and make an abode with him." When the Father and the Son come, it is not to visit; it is to make an abode. Once this dear One comes, He never goes away; He stays forever. In this same chapter the Lord says that the Spirit of reality "abides with you and shall be in you" (v. 17); He will "be with you forever" (v. 16).

Here is something extraordinary. How could God as the divine Person — holy, righteous, glorious — come into a sinful human being who is fallen, corrupted, ruined? How could He enter into us and make us His home? Such a thing could not have happened in the Old Testament. The procedure which made this possible had not yet been carried out.

THE WAY MADE POSSIBLE

The New Testament opens with the birth of God into mankind. The first thing recorded is the incarnation. That God came to be born as a man is unbelievable! But it happened. From Isaiah 9:6 we know that the little child born in a manger in Bethlehem was the mighty God. What a wonder!

The very God grew up in a poor carpenter's home. Here He passed through His childhood. We have an account of an episode when He was a child of twelve (Luke 2:41-52). For thirty years He lived there in that humble home. Then He came forth to minister. He thus sowed Himself into His followers. After three and a half years He went to the cross.

He was crucified to redeem us. As our substitute He died for us, shedding His blood for our redemption. By that death He bruised the head of the serpent; He crushed the Devil. His death released His inner, divine life. After accomplishing this work, He went into the tomb and into Hades. After three days He emerged from death and entered into resurrection.

In resurrection He took another form. No longer is He in the flesh; though He still has a physical body, it is a body in resurrection. Now in resurrection He has become a life-giving Spirit (1 Cor. 15:45). No doubt this is the Spirit of God. But before this process of incarnation, crucifixion, and resurrection the Spirit of God had no way to impart life to man. Now He is able and ready to impart the divine life into God's chosen people; thus He is indeed the life-giving Spirit. *He qualified God to impart life to people.*

Though this story has become familiar to us, it is not a simple one. God became incarnate. He was born as an infant, grew up as a child, then lived as a man, experiencing all kinds of sufferings and trials. At the cross He settled our problem with sin, with Satan, and with death. A flow of life came out of His crucified being. Then in resurrection He became this life-giving Spirit. John 7:39 says, "The Spirit was not yet, because Jesus was not yet glorified." At that time crucifixion and resurrection had not yet been accomplished; once they were, the Spirit of God was able to impart life.

Who is this life-giving Spirit? Christ. God Himself. The traditional teaching on the Trinity cannot account for all these items. Christ cannot be separated from God, nor can He be separated from the Spirit. We have the Father, the Son, and the Spirit. The Father is embodied in the Son, and the Son has become the life-giving Spirit. The way has been paved, the procedure fully carried out. Now He is ready. All that remains is for us to open and receive Him. He comes in at once.

We then have within us as our contents the very God who is the Creator and is now the dispensing Triune God. We are vessels containing the processed God. This is the mystery of Christ. Christ is the wrapping up of all the divine mysteries.

While human language is inadequate to express the things we have seen, I believe enough has been said to help you if you have a heart to see. Do not be held back by the shallow teachings. You must go on to see these deeper truths concerning God's heart's desire. Who is this indwelling God? He is the Father. He is Christ. He is the Spirit. The attempts of the theologians to systematize these truths are a failure. The reputable scholars admit that in our Christian experience Christ is identical to the Spirit. Yes, They are one; nonetheless, They are also two! Because this is a mystery, we cannot fully explain it; it corresponds, however, with our experience.

WHO CHRIST IS

The Mystery of God

In Colossians 2:2 Christ is called the mystery of God. Such a term indicates something incomprehensible and inexplicable. God is a mystery; He cannot be defined. Since the mystery of God is Christ, if we want to understand God we must understand Christ. If we want to receive God, we must receive Christ.

The Embodiment of God

Colossians 2:9 says, "For in Him dwells all the fullness of the Godhead bodily." Christ is the embodiment of God.

With Him, nothing less than God. **God**

Romans 9:5 says of Christ, "Who is over all, God blessed forever." This Christ who is the mystery of God and the embodiment of God *is* God. He is the very God! Paul clearly states this in this verse. Can Christ be separated from God? No more than you can be separated from yourself. Theologians may say that He is God the Son but not God the Father nor God the Spirit. They may have such a concept, but that is not what the Bible says. The Bible says, He is God over all. It does not say that He is only God the Son; that is an interpretation.

In Exodus 3:2 and 6 the Angel sent by Jehovah was not only the God of Abraham, but also the God of Isaac and the God of Jacob. He was not only God the Son (the God of Isaac); He was also God the Father (the God of Abraham) and God the Spirit (the God of Jacob). He is the Triune God. He cannot be separated into God the Father, God the Son, and God the Spirit. You may have such a teaching, but it is not scriptural.

We must know this Christ. He is God, the very Triune God.

A Life-giving Spirit

This One first took the step of becoming flesh (John 1:14). In the flesh He was the Lamb of God, dying for our sins to accomplish redemption. Then in resurrection He took the second step: as the last Adam, He became a life-giving Spirit (1 Cor. 15:45). Paul tells us that Christ is God Himself, the very Triune God; then he also tells us that He became a life-giving Spirit. Notice this word became. Christ took the initiative to pass from one stage to another. First He was in the stage of the flesh; after resurrection, however, He entered into the stage of the Spirit. He became a Spirit to give life to us.

There are those who claim that I have destroyed the three divine Persons of the holy Trinity. The truth is that the opposers have neglected or chosen to ignore what the Bible clearly teaches of the Trinity. While privately acknowledging that, according to Isaiah 9:6, Christ is called the Father, they dare not say this publicly because it goes against tradition.

The Spirit

"Now the Lord is the Spirit: and where the Spirit of the Lord is, there is liberty. But we all, with unveiled face beholding and reflecting as a mirror the glory of the Lord, are being transformed into the same image from glory to glory, even as from the Lord Spirit" (2 Cor. 3:17-18, lit.). No word is clearer than this: the Lord is the Spirit. Still the opposers argue that the Lord here refers to Jehovah, not to Christ. Who is Jehovah? He is Christ in the Old Testament. In the New Testament Jehovah is Jesus. Who is the Lord in verse 18, whose glory we are beholding and reflecting? Surely it can be none other than the glorious Christ, into whose image we are being transformed "even as from the Lord Spirit." Here is a compound title, Lord Spirit.

The Spirit cannot be separated from the Lord. In verse 17 we are told that the Lord is the Spirit; then we have the term Spirit of the Lord. The first part of the verse indicates that the Lord and the Spirit are one; the second part, that they are two. This is our understanding because of language. Electric current is electricity; there is no electric current apart from electricity. In the same way, the Spirit of the Lord is simply the Lord Himself.

THE TRIUNE GOD

Romans

Romans 8:9 through 11 clearly describes the Triune God. "But you are not in the flesh, but in the spirit, if indeed the Spirit of God dwells in you. But if anyone has not the Spirit of Christ, he is not of Him. And if Christ is in you, though the body is dead because of sin, yet the spirit is life because of righteousness. But if the Spirit of Him Who raised Jesus from among the dead dwells in you, He Who raised Christ Jesus from among the dead will also give life to your mortal bodies through His Spirit Who indwells you."

There is a mystery here. There is the Spirit of God, then the Spirit of Christ, then Christ. The Spirit of God is the Spirit of Christ; the Spirit of Christ is simply Christ. There is mention of God, the Spirit, and Christ. The three of the Godhead are all here. However, there are not three in us; there is only one. When we have the Spirit, we have God and Christ. When we have Christ, we have both the Spirit and God.

This God we have is not the God in Genesis 1, but the one in Romans 8, who has passed through incarnation and crucifixion and entered into resurrection. With this God we have Christ and the Spirit. The three are one and inseparable.

Ephesians

Ephesians 3:14-19 is another reference to the Triune God. "For this cause I bow my knees unto the Father, of Whom every family in the heavens and on earth is named, that He would grant you, according to the riches of His glory, to be strengthened with power through His Spirit into the inner man, that Christ may make His home in your hearts through faith, that you, having been rooted and grounded in love, may be strong to apprehend with all the saints what is the breadth and length and height and depth, and to know the knowledge-surpassing love of Christ, that you may be filled unto all the fullness of God." God the Father listens to the prayer; God the Spirit fulfills the prayer; and God the Son completes what is asked, namely, that Christ make His home in us that we be filled unto all the fullness of God. First there is the Father, then the Spirit, then Christ the Son, and finally all the fullness of God. Here is one divine Person, wrought into our being. We shall be saturated with Him, filled with Him to the brim, even running over. Then we shall become the fullness of God, expressing His riches. This is the mystery of Christ.

Second Corinthians

"The grace of the Lord Jesus Christ, and the love of God, and the fellowship of the Holy Spirit, be with you all. Amen" (2 Cor. 13:14, lit.). Here is the love of God the Father, the grace of Christ the Son, and the fellowship of God the Spirit. May all these be with you. There is such a flow to us and in us.

CLEAVING TO THE CENTRAL VISION

The central vision of the Apostle Paul's completing ministry is: God in us as our contents, Christ as the mystery of God, and the church as the mystery of Christ. We must lay aside our natural concepts whether religious, ethical, devotional, or spiritual, holy, or pious. Even the concept of having a good meeting or a strong service must not be our goal. The meetings and the service must come from the source; the church life is the issue.

The Lord's recovery is the central vision. In 1970, after the successful migrations, we began to pay attention to the spread of the recovery and became somewhat negligent of the central vision. The recovery was off, for which I have very much repented to the Lord. By His mercy He cleared things up and brought us back to the right track. The Lord has rebuked me and charged me not to do much to encourage the spreading of the recovery or to gain an increase in numbers. I am not opposed to these, but I have been charged not to be concerned about them. Let the recovery grow in life. Spontaneously there will be a spreading and a proper increase, both issuing from life, not from our doing. "Little one," the Lord pointed out, "when I was on the earth, I didn't do anything to spread my work. All I did was to sow Myself as life into a small number. Eventually in Acts 1 I had only one hundred twenty. Not many." It seems unbelievable that after the Lord's labors for three and a half years all that He reaped was a mere one hundred twenty. The Lord asked me, "From all your efforts to spread and increase, where are the one hundred twenty? After you go, where are the one hundred twenty? Who will carry on the Lord's recovery on the right track? Without the one hundred twenty, as soon as you go, everything will be off. The recovery will become a part of the pitiful history of Christianity, a repetition of its doing so many things that are scriptural and spiritual yet without Christ. If you could gain the whole world as your increase, what would that mean?"

I recently talked with the brother visiting from Taiwan. From now on, I fellowshipped with him, the work there should not pay much attention to the spreading or the increase. All your efforts must be directed toward getting the one hundred twenty. Otherwise, in ten years everything will be gone, lost because of the increase. There are already a good number in Taiwan, twenty-three thousand in the church in Taipei alone; perhaps on the whole island there are forty thousand. How many of these can be counted among the one hundred twenty? If we do not take care of this, our work will be empty concerning the central lane of God's economy. Instead of recovering, we shall be drifting back. The more spreading we have, the more we drift back to a repetition of Christianity. I am happy that there are so many, but if they do not see the central vision my happiness is futile.

We need some faithful ones to rise up and say, "Lord, here I am. Show me the central vision as you did with the Apostle Paul." I hope you younger ones, especially those who are in their twenties, will do this. Then after ten years you will be valuable to the Lord's recovery.

A message given by Witness Lee
in Anaheim, California, April 18, 1981

Published by
Living Stream Ministry
1853 W. Ball Road, Anaheim, CA 92804, U.S.A.
(714) 991-4681

THE COMPLETING MINISTRY OF PAUL

MESSAGE TWELVE

THE CENTRAL VISION

(3)

THE CHURCH AS THE MYSTERY OF CHRIST

Scripture Reading: Col. 1:25-27; Eph. 3:3-5, 9-11; 1:19-23; 4:4-6, 12-16; Col. 2:19; Rom. 12:4-5; 1 Cor. 12:12-13, 18, 27

These three messages on the Apostle Paul's completing ministry are not common. In the two previous messages we considered God and Christ, and in this message we shall consider the church. These terms themselves — God, Christ, and the church — are all too familiar. But to speak of God as our contents, Christ as God's mystery, and the church as Christ's mystery, surely is to speak in a way unfamiliar to most Christians.

THE REASON FOR THE INCARNATION

How could the almighty God, our Creator, be our contents? Even the expression is strange! For Him to be our contents He has to enter into us and take full possession of us, making our entire being His vessel. This may sound simple. We may think that if God wants to do something, He simply does it. Such is not the case. God had to be triune in order to work Himself into our being. There was a procedure He had to pass through in order to have a way to enter into us. This is a most profound matter. It explains why the almighty God became incarnate.

God was born into man. He was born of humanity to be a man. The very God lived on this earth in a poor carpenter's home for thirty years. Then day after day He stayed with His disciples to pass on the divine economy to those earthly human beings. His way of teaching was altogether different from that of Socrates, Plato, or Confucius.

After He had stayed with them more than three years, He suddenly told them He was going away (John 13:33). This troubled them. He went on to say that He would not leave them for good, or even for a long period of time. He would not desert them by leaving them orphans; He would be gone just for a short period of three days. He would go through the process of being crucified, buried, and resurrected, so that He might be changed into another form, that of the life-giving Spirit (1 Cor. 15:45). By this means He could not only come back to be with them; He would be able to enter into them that He might abide in them and they in Him. He told the disciples clearly that He was going away to prepare a place, to pave a way, to gain the ground, for them to be brought into the Father.

These words that He spoke to the disciples in John 14 have been altogether misinterpreted. The common explanation is that the Lord Jesus told His disciples He was going to leave them, to die and go to heaven, and there He would prepare heavenly mansions for them. When they were finished, He would come back for the disciples and receive them into those mansions. What a tragedy to interpret the Lord's word in this way!

RETURNING IN RESURRECTION

Actually His going was His coming back. His leaving them was His walking into them. By taking a few steps He entered into them. What were these steps? His death, burial, and resurrection. He returned to them on the third day, not in His original form, but like breath, in the form of the Spirit. What we are saying is elusive and mysterious. Christ is a mystery. Do you think He came back physically after His resurrection? If so, how could He enter the room where the disciples were meeting with the doors shut? He did not knock on the door and ask them to let Him in. While they were meeting together, sorrowful and grieving, wondering what to do, wondering where His body had been taken, He Himself came and stood in their midst. If you believe His coming here was spiritual, how could He have asked Thomas to touch His hands and put his hand into His side (John 20:27)? Theologians, were these appearances spiritual or physical? There is no way to come to a conclusion.

He may have been standing there for quite a while, listening to the words of those pitiful, frightened disciples. In any case, suddenly He became visible to them. He said, "Peace be to you" (John 20:19); there was no need for them to be troubled. Then He breathed into them and said, "Receive the holy *pneuma*." *Pneuma* means both breath and spirit. By inhaling His breath, the disciples received Him as the Spirit. They had no choice. They were in the same room. They had to keep breathing to stay alive. By inhaling what He breathed out, the disciples experienced His entering into them.

THE LORD'S ABIDING PRESENCE

Did He leave after that? No! There is the record of His appearing among them, but nothing is said as to His leaving. He remained with them. Where? He was *in* them. Once the Lord Jesus entered into them, He never left. If you read John 20 and 21 carefully, you will see that the disciples, including Peter, did not realize this. When He disappeared from sight, He was still with them.

After some time Peter evidently felt he could not tolerate this way of living; he decided to go fishing. The others followed him, since he was their leader. They were not the only ones following; the Lord Himself was following too in each one of them. They fished and fished, but their efforts were futile. Not one fish did they catch. Then the Lord Jesus said to them from the shore, "Cast the net on the right side of the boat" (21:6), and when they did, they had more fish than they could handle. Then they recognized who it was who had spoken to them from the shore.

This story shows how the Lord trained the disciples to appreciate His invisible presence within them more than

His external presence among them before His death. This Jesus was now within them.

THE INDWELLING ONE

Who was this One who got into them? The almighty Creator, the Triune God Himself. The Son of God was not separated from the Father. Where the Son was, the Father was also. The same is true of the Spirit: where the Spirit was, the Son was also. Thus, the One who entered into the disciples was the very Triune God. He was not merely the Creator described in Genesis 1. By now He had gone through the process of incarnation, crucifixion, and resurrection.

How qualified and equipped He was to enter into man! He had accomplished redemption. He had destroyed death. He had defeated the Devil. He had released His life. He had become the available, life-giving breath, *pneuma*, Spirit. Satan might say, "God, You cannot enter into these sinful human beings," but God would reply, "Yes, they were sinful, but I have redeemed them. My blood was shed for them. Let them be! You have been defeated. You have no ground to speak against them. The full liberty is Mine to enter into them!"

This One is the Spirit of God, the Spirit of Christ, and the indwelling Christ. This realization goes far deeper than what is commonly understood of Christ's incarnation, death, and resurrection. Many Christians have only an objective, superficial belief that we were fallen sinners; that God the Father loved the world and sent His Son to be our Savior and Redeemer; that He came as the Lamb of God and died on the cross for our sins; that He was buried; that after three days He was resurrected; that He ascended to heaven and is now seated on the throne; that He sent down the Holy Spirit as His instrument to inspire sinners to repent and believe in Him; that this Holy Spirit as the Representative of the Christ in heaven indwells those who thus believe; that when we have problems we pray to the Father about them; that our Mediator is there on the throne praying for us, taking care of our case and seeing that our prayers are answered.

To think in this way is not wrong, but it is superficial. It also borders on believing that there are three Gods. In the Vatican there is a floor-to-ceiling painting depicting an old father with a long white beard, a young son standing nearby, and a dove hovering overhead. Such is their concept of the Trinity! Alongside is another painting, with an extra person added. Besides the father, the son, and the dove, there is a young woman, supposedly the son's mother, the mother of God! This is their God! How repulsive! It shows an ignorance of God's economy to dispense Himself into His redeemed people by being triune.

Christ is a mystery. While He is abiding in you, He is still seated on the throne. When He comes to you, He comes with both the Father and the Spirit. When one comes, all three come. This is what triune means. We cannot explain the Godhead. But then, there are things about electricity that we cannot understand either; nonetheless, when we turn on the current, we can utilize its power. The Triune God cannot be fully understood. He is called Wonderful (Isa. 9:6) for this very reason. He is a totality of wonder, a mystery impossible to comprehend. This is true more than ever, now that He has gone through incarnation, crucifixion, and resurrection. There is divinity in Him. There is humanity in Him. There is human life in Him. Who can understand such a One? This is the very One who is within us to be our contents. Some may say that our teaching is heretical, but it is altogether according to the divine revelation in the Bible.

The Issue

THE INDWELLING TO PRODUCE THE BODY

What is the issue of God's entering into us? It is the Body of Christ. This is also mysterious. To have the church as the Body of Christ, as Ephesians 1 tells us, involves Christ's resurrection, His ascension, and His headship. It was the divine power which raised Christ from the dead, uplifted Him to the heavens, and made Him Head over all things to the church. The Body of Christ is produced by His ascension and headship.

If the church were simply an assembly of Christ's believers, there would probably be no need for so many factors to be involved. But for the church to be the Body of Christ is not a simple matter. Even for us to have a physical body is not simple. Yes, we can have false teeth and artificial limbs, but to organically produce a member of the body is another matter. Perhaps a transplant is the best modern medicine can do.

Who can make us dead human beings part of Christ's living Body? The crucified, resurrected, ascended Christ can! We are not like false teeth; we are organically part of the Body. The Creator could create us as human beings, but without passing through a process even He could not make us organically part of the Body of Christ. He first had to be incarnated, crucified, and resurrected in order to be qualified to make us the living members of His Body. Creative power was not adequate. It took Jesus Christ — the incarnated, crucified, resurrected One, the One who has been made Head over all — to accomplish this. Because He is now within us, we have become organically members of His Body.

We are also members one of another. The arm and the shoulder, as joint members, are related organically to each other. The building up of the Body is the growing together of the members. The hand is built with the arm and the arm with the shoulder. The relationship is not mechanical like a robot. We do not function in the church like robots, regulated and controlled by the elders. Do we function in the meetings because we are told to by the elders? Do we come to the Saturday morning service because they have told us we should? We are not parts of a mechanical being but living members of an organism! This living organism is being produced, not by a creative act, but by the qualified Christ. Whatever He has gone through, whatever He has obtained and attained, whatever He has entered into, is all for the producing of His Body. Ephesians 1:19-23 makes this clear.

In Ephesians 3 the church is called the mystery of Christ (v. 4). Christ is the mystery of God; similarly, the church, this organic entity, is the mystery of Christ. It was purposed, planned, and designed in eternity.

In Ephesians 4:4-6 it is clear that the Body is wrapped up with the Triune God. "One Body and one Spirit, as also you were called in one hope of your calling; one Lord, one faith, one baptism; one God and Father of all, Who is over all and through all and in all." There is one Body, one Spirit, one Lord, and one God and Father. All three of the Godhead are blended with the Body. Just as we cannot separate the three of the Godhead, neither can we separate the church as the Body from the three. They are blended together.

Some object to our saying that we are mingled with God. In the preface to Darby's *New Translation*, Darby comments on the difficulty of using a large or small s for the word spirit when it is not clear whether the Holy Spirit or our spirit is meant. Three times in this one paragraph Darby uses the word blended. He says that the way spirit is used indicates our state. That is, God as the Spirit is blended with our spirit; this is the state we are in.

Hallelujah that the divine Spirit, having passed through so many processes, has become one spirit with us! Christians like to hear about miracles. Surely this is the top miracle: that God has gone through so much and has accomplished so much that He is fully equipped to be blended with us! What a state we are in! We are the living members of the organic Body of Christ.

The topmiracle, miracle of miracles!

THE BODY MENTIONED ONLY BY PAUL

There is only one writer in the Bible who tells us of the Body of Christ. The Old Testament writers saw nothing of it. It was a mystery hidden from them. The mystery of Christ, which is His Body, has been made manifest only in the New Testament age. Yet only Paul refers to it. Peter does not. Nor does John, even though his mending ministry was to bring the saints back to Paul's completing ministry. Even in Paul's writings, only four of his fourteen Epistles speak of the Body of Christ; the other ten do not mention it. Romans, 1 Corinthians, Ephesians, and Colossians are the only books that refer to the Body of Christ. I tried to see if there is a hint anywhere as to where Paul might have picked up the thought of the Body of Christ. I could not find a hint. Paul received a unique vision that the church is the Body of Christ.

This revelation has been lost, overlooked, or neglected by Christians. Consider all the practices that came in after the reformation. There were the practices of the Puritans, of the Mennonites, of the Amish, and of the various kinds of Brethren. In Germany there were different kinds of Orders with their particular rules. Then there were the Presbyterians with their practice and the Baptists with theirs. I must tell you that no matter what practices you follow or what kind of Brethren or Order you belong to, these groups are not the Body. All these practices are off.

When I was in Ohio, I visited an Amish community. I saw nothing of Christ. I saw old wagons. I saw drab clothing; they could wear only black, white, gray, and dark blue. Such practices are other than Christ.

Nowadays the term communal life has been popularized. Even to have a communal life based on Acts 2:44-45 is not the Body. When Paul got saved, the communal life was over. Even by Acts 6 the communal life was almost over because of the murmurings. Then Paul came on the scene. He told the Corinthians to bring their offerings to the church meetings on the Lord's Day to take care of others (1 Cor. 16:1-2). Here is a strong indication that communal living was at an end. There may be a communal life without the Body of Christ. A communal life can be set up, but not so with the Body of Christ. The Body requires the resurrection, ascension, and headship of Christ.

In 1933 some young men from the British Navy who were with the Brethren in England heard of our meeting in

Shanghai and came to visit us. They were well trained. They knew how to baptize, who could baptize, whom to baptize, and how to accept a believer at the Lord's table. I was young then, only about twenty-eight. I admired them and thought we should learn of them; they were so clear about how things ought to be.

A LIVING BODY, NOT A ROBOT

Now I think differently. That kind of knowledge is helpful only to a robot. A mechanical man is programmed to know just what to do. A living person, in contrast, is not quite sure. He does not know what is best for his situation. He does not know what to do, but he is living! Suppose you are asked how we baptize people and whom we accept at the Lord's table. If you have a ready answer to every question, you are acting like a robot. If you simply reply, "We have no way. We just walk according to spirit," they will press you further. "Do you mean the Holy Spirit?" When you explain that you are referring to the mingled spirit, they will ask, "What? Mingled spirit? What is that? We want to know how you have the Lord's table. Do you use leavened or unleavened bread? Do you have wine or grape juice?" If you say, "I have nothing to tell you. We simply seek to walk according to spirit," you can be sure they will be through with you.

Is not today's Christianity made up of robots? Look at the pitiful robots belonging to the Catholic Church, the small robots following the big ones. There are cardinal robots and archbishop robots. Is the Lord's recovery like this? I am concerned about this question. We must not make the saints robots.

The Body is an organism. We are organic members of this organism, not robots. Read again the description in Ephesians 4:12-16. The Body is built up directly by every member. Verse 16 says, "Out from Whom all the Body, fitted and knit together through every joint of the supply, according to the operation in measure of each one part, causes the growth of the Body unto the building up of itself in love."

You may have an evangelical work but with no intention to build up the Body. You may have a communal life, but that may not be the Body. For the Body to be built up, you must first have a clear vision of the Body. (Then as you live in the Body, you will grow. That growth of yours spontaneously builds the Body.) Verse 16 says that all the members grow to build up the Body (cf. also Col. 2:19).

When will the Lord gain what He is after? There is a groaning in me about this. Not only is there a lacking of the Body life; even the meaning of the words is misunderstood. Nonetheless, the Lord has His way. The way is organic. It is by life, and life is through death and resurrection. We all need to see this central point of Paul's completing ministry.

THE BODY IN ROMANS

"For as in one body we have many members, and all the members do not have the same function, so we being many, are one body in Christ, and severally members one of another" (Rom. 12:4-5).

In Romans 12 what is said about the Body is quite simple. This is because Romans 12 is preceded by Romans 8, which is surely not simple! What do we find in Romans 8? There is death and resurrection. There is the Triune God in death and resurrection all wrapped up with the tripartite man. There is the Spirit of God, the Spirit of Christ, then Christ. God, Christ, the Spirit — with His death and resurrection — now indwells us, to make our spirit life (v. 10), to make our mind life (v. 6), and to make even our mortal body life (v. 13). Is this not a mingling? Is this not an organic wrapping up of the Triune God and us, the tripartite man? I tell you, this is the way the members of the Body will be produced.

THE BODY IN FIRST CORINTHIANS

"For even as the body is one and has many members,

but all the members of the body being many are one body, so also is Christ; for also in one Spirit we were all baptized into one body, whether Jews or Greeks, whether slaves or free, and were all given to drink one Spirit. But now God has set the members, every one of them, in the body, even as He willed. Now you are the body of Christ, and members in particular" (1 Cor. 12:12-13, 18, 27).

These verses tell us that this organic Body is also Christ, the corporate Christ. All the members have been baptized in one Spirit into one Body. The Body, then, is altogether something in the Spirit.

WHAT THE LORD IS AFTER

In summary I remind you of these three crucial points in Paul's Epistles: God as our contents, Christ as God's mystery, and the church as Christ's mystery. Without these three points, Paul's writings are an empty shell. These are what the Lord is going to recover. Without them, nothing is meaningful. Our God today is in us to be our contents. The mystery of God is Christ as the embodiment and manifestation of God, making God so real and so enjoyable to us. The mystery of Christ is that the Triune God through death and in resurrection is mingling Himself with us, making us the living members of His organic Body. This vision must direct us. It will keep us in the central lane, walking according to the mingled spirit and being in the Body life. This is what the Lord is after.

A message given by Witness Lee
in Anaheim, California, April 18, 1981

© 1981 Living Stream Ministry

Published by
Living Stream Ministry
1853 W. Ball Road, Anaheim, CA 92804, U.S.A.
(714) 991-4681